D1553711

# Where's Jimmy?

*A Lifetime Search for a Little Boy's Soul
and the Discovery of My Own*

Kathy Jefford

ISBN: 9798491901951

SUMMARY: Inspired to search for the soul of a little boy and to discover her own beliefs when the impact of her family's beliefs shatters her world.

Editor, supporter, and cheerleader: Andria Flores (andriaflores17@gmail.com)

Reader, collaborator, and friend: Sonya Brown

Artist: Jan O'Dea

Cover designer: Jen Aiken (jen@jvodesign.com)

All events described in this book are shared genuinely through the perceptions of the author.

# Table of Contents

# Introduction

My story unfolds as a young girl in a strict religious community who was stunned by the sudden loss and the shaming that followed as I grasped to understand the fate of my childhood companion, Jimmy. The first chapters are to a certain extent awkward, much like an eight-year-old little girl would be as she fumbles to recount and reconcile complex situations and simply longs for comfort and connection from the adults in her life. In reflection, my heart breaks for the naïve child and young adult I was seeking security and peace to remedy the confusion and chaos in my life.

While my story reveals my personal experience with the immovable religious beliefs of my father in the Jehovah's Witness community in which I was raised, I acknowledge that other believers have their own spiritual experiences that will certainly differ from mine. I was taught that I was a chosen one, that I was special. Therefore I was expected to live distinctively and set apart from my peers at school and in my interactions with non-believers, or those who had not been chosen. At an impressionable age when children celebrate birthdays and holidays with gifts or color seasonal images and sing songs, I was not permitted to acknowledge my birthdate, much less participate in traditional celebrations of such events. Rather, I was often banished to the school hallway at my father's adamant instruction, when all I wanted was to just be a regular girl. The impact of my family's spiritual beliefs, some virtuous and some destructive, fashioned a lens through which I perceived life and all of its opportunities and choices.

I believe that when the student is ready the teacher appears, and when the reader is ready the book appears. For me, inspiration came after reading ***Hillbilly Elegy, A Memoir of a Family and Culture in Crisis*** by J. D. Vance and ***Educated, A Memoir*** by Tara Westover. That's when I became compelled to write for readers who might connect with my story. To quote J. D. Vance in his introduction, *"I want people to know what it feels like to nearly give up on yourself and why you might do it."* And to quote Tara Westover, *"**Educated** is an account of the struggle for self-invention. It is a tale…of the grief that comes from severing one's closest ties."* Both authors inspired me with their honesty, loyalty, and accomplishments.

I hope you will be moved toward understanding and compassion—both for yourself and others—as you read my account. I humbly invite you to walk through the discomfort, dysfunction, and desperation of my youth, as I mature enough to unlock a heart full of questions. The truth is I spent a lifetime looking for more than answers, more than Jimmy, even more than myself. I have been seeking hope. And upon finding it, now my desire is to inspire hope and love and compassion for you, regardless where your spiritual journey begins and ends.

Warmest regards,
Kathy

# I

# Where's Jimmy?

Bright colors and drawings of flowers, beautiful as works of art, attracted me to the packages of seeds in the late winter and early spring. My grandmother carefully studied the packages of vegetable seeds, vital food for her family. Flowers were a luxury and not essential for us. Still I did not realize at the time that we were poor. Counting my pennies, I selected a package of bright blues, my favorite color! That day, Bachelor Button flowers would replace my standard purchase of the penny candy I so loved.

My life is a tapestry woven with many threads, as Carole King sang, "an everlasting vision of the ever-changing view." Threads of dissonance and inharmonious beliefs search for a song of harmony, compassion, and sweet understanding I imagine…

*A beautiful mountain scene where white fluffy clouds float gently amid the deep rich blue sky, the immense quiet, save an eagle's chance high-pitched whistle. Jimmy walks and plays in the sun laughing sweetly, innocently, collecting rocks flecked with gold, blue columbine, and alpine flowers. Running and rolling in the grass, unafraid to fall or bruise, he is as healthy and strong as the land. Watching fish swim beneath the mirror of a calm mountain lake, he holds my hand to pull me up. Then he climbs around the next switchback along the path into a clearing, stopping to breathe, to inhale pure air. He turns his face upward to the sun for warmth and light at midday. No shadows darken the moments. A gentle wind blows the occasional wisp of cloud moving softly, effortlessly over to the next valley or peak, feeling light as a feather. There is no worry or pain. Happiness is the feeling we share.*

As a young girl, early springs were spent digging in the family garden with my paternal grandmother, touching the soft crumbling dirt prepared to receive seeds saved from last year. Blue Bachelor Buttons, bright yellow and orange marigolds, and pretty petunias promised vibrant colors to border the multihued greens from the grass and abundant vegetable garden in late spring, summer, and early fall. The fragrance of peonies and roses embed memories of warmer, sunnier days.

Planting in April, we watched expectantly for flowers blooming in June to paint our yards and make bouquets for kitchens and picnic tables. Mason jars full of flowers adorned countertops full of fried chicken, potato salads, cole slaw, watermelon, lemonade and fruit pies. These were halcyon days taken for granted before turbulent times would appear.

My mother, the world's best pie, cake, and cookie baker always served fresh baked desserts after dinner and for snacks during the day. As my sweet tooth developed, I pleaded for more sugary delights. For two years Jimmy's mother offered endless little red boxes of raisins for our snacks. Raisins were good for him to build up his blood cells and make him healthy, so I ate raisins with Jimmy while secretly wishing for sweeter delights.

My only friend, Jimmy, at the age of two had leukemia. His mother would pick me up from our modest mobile home and take me to their basement home to play with him. Hearing his wholehearted, free-of-pain giggle, filled me with happiness. Buffering him to prevent falls and cuts or bruises often meant his annoyance with me. His face swollen from his medicine, likely steroids, told me he was not well and needed laughter and diversion to ease his pain. I was his chosen big sister and babysitter, almost four years older, assigned to protect, play, and entertain him indoors. Both of us preferred to be outdoors in the sunshine, rain, or snow, or really in any weather, even with its inherent dangers. Splashing in mud puddles could be fun too. At times, I was jealous of him always getting his way. When I protested, I was again reminded of his fragile health and so vowed to keep him safe and smiling.

With identical small black and white stuffed teddy bears, always at our sides, Jimmy and I ran Matchbox cars and trucks across the floors, filling hours of play time. His mother picked me up on her way home from work as a nurse to visit and play with him as often as possible. Their basement home, being built in stages, had yet to begin construction of the first floor. Rugs covered the cement basement floors making it hard to roll toy cars and trucks. Switching to plastic cowboys, horses, and fences, Roy Rogers and Dale Evans were difficult to keep standing. Well-padded soft rugs kept toppling toys for ranches and Wild West scenes. Cardboard boxes for barns and buildings offered horses and cowboys a place to stand upright.

*The month of June brings misty summer raindrops mingled with tears quietly rolling down my cheeks. Do angels weep tears of sadness when babies die? Do they shed tears of joy to hold them close? Do we shed tears of joy to hold them in sweet memory?*

My father, mother, sisters, and two-month-old baby brother slowly moved past Jimmy's small casket before they took seats in the funeral parlor. I hung back last, hesitantly wanting to see and touch Jimmy, only four years old, to waken his still body. His mother gently nudged me and slowly lifted the shiny white satin blanket covering his legs. She whispered, "This is our secret." Barely tall enough to peek inside, I saw his small black and white Teddy Bear, identical to mine, and I smiled a little. A little red box of Sun-Maid raisins brought another grin, maybe not as sweet, remembering the countless times we ate them together. "Raisins build up the blood," I recalled hearing and frowned wondering why they didn't work. A photo of his parents and family and a few easily hidden tiny toys rounded out the secret stash.

The satin blanket then quickly returned to hide the hidden treasures from view of those who would criticize and condemn his mother. Mean old women would judge her tiny gifts as senseless. To them, the dead are not aware of anything. *Why do they fail to see the comfort to those still alive?* Jimmy's kind, devastated father, unable to speak and barely able to stand at the head of casket, meekly anchored himself to protect and defend his only child. I had not been allowed to see Jimmy for a while before he died at home. *How do a mother and father survive watching life leave their precious and beloved son?*

I was taught that Jimmy would be resurrected into a Paradise earth when the wicked were destroyed. Everyone, perfectly healthy and living forever, was the promise after death. Different from many who believed in a fiery place of torment, my father's religious conviction did not believe in hell. Different from those who believed heaven to be peaceful and soft as clouds, I was taught Jimmy would not go to heaven. My father said only 144,000 chosen, faithful followers of Jehovah went to heaven—a small number compared to the billions now alive and the billions who have died. I was comforted in the belief that I would play with Jimmy again on a Paradise earth.

It was 1962 and strongly believed among Jehovah's Witnesses that in only 13 years, in 1975, the war of Armageddon would destroy all wicked people who were not Jehovah's faithful Witnesses. The faithful living Witnesses and those resurrected would joyously work to restore the earth to the Paradise given to Adam and Eve. Thirteen years seemed a long time to an eight-year-old girl, but I had confidence Jimmy and I would play together again.

In the year or two that followed his death, Jimmy's parents gradually stopped participating in the religion. Their loss of faith was obvious when they did not attend the five weekly meetings or preach door-to-door. Whispered conversations from old women in the Kingdom Hall exaggerated rhetoric of the fate of Jimmy now that his parents were no longer faithful Witnesses. His parents eventually divorced, as often happens after the serious illness or death of a child. Divorce brought the final verdict of Jimmy's assumed fate according to the gossipers. Divorce was only allowed on the grounds of adultery, a word I did not understand then. Never knowing if adultery was the reason didn't seem to matter. The parents, and with them, Jimmy, were now the wicked who would not have God's favor. No Paradise for them - simply dust-to-dust, forever lost, and forever to be forgotten, and not spoken of again.

Heartbroken upon hearing the judgmental verdicts from conversations of hateful busybodies, I pleaded with my father, "Please tell me Jimmy will be resurrected, and I will be with him again." I needed assurance God still loved Jimmy and would remember and resurrect him. My father said, "Jehovah tells us what He expects of His faithful ones, and if they do not obey, Jimmy will not be resurrected." He could not give that which I pleaded for and needed to hear. *How could Jimmy, a sweet four-year-old, be forgotten and deemed worthless by a god who was supposed to love?*

Two years before his death, on my first day of school, other doubts emerged that questioned my father's beliefs. My mind reasoned, *who deserves comfort and relief more than a four-year-old, ill with the pain and suffering of leukemia or any illness?* Overhearing conversations of people debating what happens to Jimmy after his death fostered even greater confusion and dismay. I heard, "Jimmy is not old enough to decide to dedicate his life to Jehovah through baptism, so he will not be in Paradise." And others stated, "It is up to the faithfulness of his parents to ensure God will place him in Paradise." Since his parents didn't allow him to take blood transfusions, forbidden by their beliefs, they were at one time hailed as faithful. It was little comfort to discover years later that at the time of his death there was no cure for leukemia. Even if he was given blood transfusions, he would not have survived the merciless disease. *Why didn't their faithfulness count for something? How could their God decide this sweet, innocent boy was meaningless and of no value?*

I was acquainted with only two very old women, a mother and her old maid daughter who claimed the distinction of being chosen ones of the 144,000 going to heaven. Asking my father how these women knew they were chosen, and why neither I nor Jimmy would be chosen, brought his annoyance. According to the teaching, only men went to heaven and became kings and princes—a fact avoided and never directly addressed. I kept questioning more of his beliefs, and ultimately his God. Questioning was paramount to wickedness. I was told, "Some questions cannot be answered because man cannot understand the mind of God." I was instructed, "Believe without doubt. Be faithful. And do not ask questions to confuse others." My voice became mute, but my mind screamed with questions of contradictory beliefs. "Doubt is as evil as critical thinking." *But how does one stop one's mind from thinking, doubting, and questioning?*

Almost sixty years later, I relayed the story of Jimmy to a work friend, Chris. She shared, "My religion teaches that all little children go to heaven when they die, no matter what." Her belief is a beautiful comfort and would have been welcomed so many years ago. Even though I do not believe in heaven or hell, the idea of Jimmy being welcomed is a lovely thought. Maybe there is a loving god or spirit who is not the punitive god I was raised to believe in.

Where is Jimmy? For over sixty years, he has been ever alive in my memory and life's search for truth.

# 2

## First Grade

Excitedly, I waited for my father to come home after my first day at a small rural public school. "Daddy," I said, "my teacher and all the students are so nice." My father reminded me, "Your teacher and all the children are wicked and will die in Armageddon, unless they become Jehovah's Witnesses. You must always be an example to them of Jehovah's chosen ones and preach to them the good news of his kingdom."

He told me I had to show how happy and proud I was to be one of Jehovah's Witnesses. Otherwise, why would anyone want to become a part of something unhappy?

The second day of school, with shoulders carrying a heavy burden, I looked at my teacher and classmates differently. My depression undoubtedly started then and would frequently, if not consistently, be present much of my life. My father had demanded of me, "Do not cry, cry out, yell, scream, or speak loudly. You must be perfectly calm and discreet." His expectations were not in my real nature, so I found ways to be funny in hopes my classmates might warm up to me and like me.

Some may find it difficult to believe a young child could even think these thoughts. My father bragged, "I read the Bible to you and spoke to you in the womb." Every Witness was required to attend five one-hour meetings every week, regardless of age, where we heard about Jehovah, Armageddon, Paradise and all the beliefs. Besides meetings, as I grew and learned to read, I was required to read their Bible, four magazines a month, endless books, and study the material for the weekly meetings. The mountain of information I was force-fed allowed little time for anything else.

Besides meetings in the local congregation there were also regional assemblies on weekends and national assemblies where new books were regularly released. Before the release of a new book there was much excitement and expectation of wonderful new information for believers to digest. I remember lining up to purchase my own copy of a new book and excitedly reading my very own copy. Witnesses were to get the new book into the hands of non-Witnesses by going door-to-door. During assemblies held in large cities we stood on street corners "hawking" literature and wearing placards to advertise the event.

I believe the man who started the belief-system and doctrine was or became a publisher. How smart he was to print his own Bible, books, magazines, calendars, and other printed material to be required purchases for the personal use of his followers and to be placed with non-believers at their homes. It seems to be quite a business model.

One image seared in my mind is the cover of a Watchtower magazine I saw as a child: the faces of terrified people fleeing, as behind them churches and government buildings were being destroyed, and they knew they would also be destroyed. The images of the people who were destroyed were those of my neighbors, classmates and relatives who were not Witnesses. It was frightening and very real.

Setting an example to the other children at school included not saluting the American flag, not coloring pictures of anything related to Thanksgiving, Christmas, Valentine's Day, Easter, Presidents Day, or other US government holidays. I could not sing Christmas carols or Happy Birthday or eat cake brought to celebrate my peers' birthdays. I was quickly labeled by fellow students, "unpatriotic, weird, odd, a goody-two-shoes." Many of my days in elementary school were spent sitting in the alcove of the principal's office as my father had instructed my teachers in advance to keep me far away from the evil celebrations. He assured me that he was protecting me from learning wicked ways. Sometimes a kind teacher would give me a picture of spring flowers to color when other children colored an Easter egg, or a snowman when others colored decorated Christmas trees so I could at least stay in the classroom. When I sat silent in the alcove I overheard other students laughing, singing carols, eating cake and treats and exchanging gifts. I was embarrassed to leave the classroom and I felt so different and lonely. I felt like an outcast even though my father told me I should feel proud to be a special chosen one of Jehovah. I wanted to sing and decorate and receive gifts. Getting new school supplies each year was the closest I came to having presents as a child.

Without birthdays and holiday celebrations, I never received presents, so I could not even lie when school resumed after Christmas Break, and students spoke excitedly of their new gifts. I had none. It was embarrassing not to have anything to share. Some students looked at me with pity and others looked at me with frowns. Did they think I was bad and not on Santa's good list? After all, I was often in the chair by the principal's office. Likewise, Show and Tell any time during the school year caused me to worry as I didn't usually have anything to show. I do remember my cat had one kitten which I could tell about but not show. My cat almost died and I begged my mother to take it to the vet. She did only to suffer later because my father berated her for doing so.

Junior high school merged several elementary schools which provided me an opportunity to interact with students who didn't know my background. I was accepted by many simply based on being another regular student. There were sports and clubs in which I wanted to participate but was not permitted by my father. I was able to play basketball only at lunch which was fun and I felt free during the game. For one class we were to dress up as a character and I was given Ares, the Greek god of war. I asked my mother to help make a costume and she was sympathetic but we knew my father would never allow it. I took a roll of aluminum foil to school and wrapped it around my arms, legs and body so I could have makeshift armor.

The elementary schools I attended were in all white neighborhoods. There were no black Witnesses in the local congregation but there were some in neighboring congregations. So when I reached junior high and schools were combined there were black students. Most teachers sat students in alphabetic order so I made friends with some black students who were seated near me in several classes and who didn't know I was a Witness. I remember Lee, Michelle and Norman fondly for their friendships during school hours. I knew better than to share information about them with my father.

My father was prejudiced against blacks and other races. His racism was evident more by what he didn't say or do than what he did. As a Witness he was expected to accept all Witness members regardless of race. There was a tradition among

Witnesses when I was growing up that occurred as the children of Witnesses reached their teens. The parents of new teen would host gatherings of teenagers from congregations within a thirty to fifty mile radius. Even expanding that far there were usually fewer than twenty or so teenagers who attended the get-togethers. The parents' goal was to find potential future mates who were Witnesses. At one event there were new members who were black. I gravitated toward them and my father noticed. He let me know in no uncertain terms that I could not date them. I was told that my father said he would rather his son marry a man than a black woman. Of course, Witnesses preached against homosexuality, so this was an unspoken family secret and another inconsistency in his beliefs.

High school merged even more schools and presented still more students who didn't know me. I was able to join the radio news club as it was held mostly during regular school hours. I liked being a reporter but I was limited to story topics and events as I was not permitted to attend after school events. Neither could I attend school dances or proms. My mother's little brother was the high school football coach. Mom opposed her husband and took us to a high school football game to watch him. I loved it.

One of my greatest blessings was that none of Mom's family were Witnesses. I was allowed to visit one of her sisters, who lived about two hours away, for a week in the summer. I loved every minute of her acceptance and my freedom from worrying with the exception that I was required to attend meetings at the Kingdom Hall in their town even though I knew no one. I wished and dreamed I was allowed to always live with them. My life would have taken a very different course.

Thankfully, my mother loved playing board games and card games like Euchre and Rummy and she would buy them for us as a family. I suspect not celebrating birthdays was designed to limit individuality more than it could be attributed to a lack of money. Members were cogs in the wheel of the Watchtower organization. I was taught there were two birthday celebrations in the Bible where someone was killed. In the Old Testament, Pharaoh had someone killed on his birthday, and in the New Testament, Herod had John the Baptist killed during Herod's birthday celebration. It always seemed a pretty lame reason not to celebrate the birth of children.

I recently looked to see if the organization still teaches the same belief today. I found that they still teach birthdays are connected to evil spirits, horoscopes, and astrology. However, I am not surprised to see another string of new thinking, as they encourage giving children gifts, just not on their birthdays. My parents never said happy birthday and never gave us parties or gifts. My mother simply told us how old we were every year on our birthday. To be fair, when I was ten years old my father did buy me a bicycle after months of pleading.

Speaking of evil spirits, I was not allowed to watch Casper the Friendly Ghost or Bewitched or many other shows and movies as they were considered dangerous. I was told Satan and his demons could enter my mind and I could be led astray from Jehovah. I was told that Satan and his demons evil activity has increased since they were thrown out of heaven. Reports were cited from around the world of their cruelty and how they afflict some people with illness. Evil spirits harass at night, depriving of sleep or giving terrible dreams, can abuse sexually and can drive people to insanity, murder, or suicide. What terrifying thoughts for an adult and even more so for a child. We were taught to repeatedly to say the name *Jehovah* out loud if we were ever confronted by evil spirits.

During nearly all of my childhood I was protected from the world, which was considered anyone who was not a Witness. At one time, all of our neighbors on a few acres of land were Witnesses who watched with judgmental eyes for any missteps. We lived in a modest mobile home outside of town on a hill with other families of Witnesses. It was an organized, almost closed, community based on the residents' religious beliefs. Save the few times I could visit my mother's family, I had little contact with non-Witnesses or worldly people.

I lived an often sad and lonely life as judgmental eyes of Witness-neighbors sought to find fault. Many Witnesses seemed to enjoy being tattletales, a term generally thought of among children. Was it a tool to inform elders of the mistakes of others in order to redirect attention from their own mistakes? Like a magician draws an audience's attention to one area in order to distract from another, it's ultimately a form of deception.

Later, when I entered the world of personnel management, I recognized that employees who told on others were the real people I really needed to watch.

Looking back I am glad I was able to attend public schools. Being home schooled with only the association of other Witnesses would have provided a terribly limited education.

# 3

# Preaching Door-to-Door

For my father, attending meetings of Jehovah's Witnesses and preaching door-to-door were the most, if not nearly the only, important activities in life. Family was only important to the extent each person was a faithful Witness. My father expected perfection from his wife and children and only gave praise for giving a right answer during a meeting or leaving literature with worldly people by going door-to-door. Getting a good report card or being on the honor roll at school held little to no value, except that I was successfully able to read the Bible and Witness' literature.

At four or five years old, my father paraded me to houses to read, or rather pretend to read a memorized scripture holding a Bible at the door with him. I received a rare smile from him when the person at the home paused to listen to me and then his spiel, maybe even a pat on the head when someone accepted literature. Being used became part of my day-to-day existence.

In 1953, the year I was born, my father attended an international assembly of over 100,000 Jehovah's Witnesses at Yankee Stadium in New York City. During the eight-day event, their report of the New World Society of Jehovah's Witnesses featured a new Bible highlighting the name *Jehovah*. New books titled Make Sure of All Things and New Heavens and New Earth were released as well as magazines and printed tracts. Years later I saw a photograph of a young boy at an assembly handing out an invitation to a non-Witness for a free Bible talk or lecture. Using children to promote their message was expected and praised.

The Watch Tower Society provided many sessions for training to preach, and my father believed every word, most especially the consistent threat of a fiery death at Armageddon, which they taught, awaits anyone who is not one of Jehovah's Witnesses. The threat is constantly reinforced in their literature, through words and illustrations. The theme is also included in literature for children, who grow up with an endless threat of death looming over their heads. Is this a form of child abuse?

I hated going door-to-door. Years ago a Witness would receive a tiny map pasted on a card, likely cut from a city or county map. Each Witness was expected to knock on every door and notate if someone accepted literature, and then return to the person at home to take more literature with a goal to get them to a Bible study and to the Kingdom Hall. If someone was not home, it was noted and the Witness was expected to return until someone answered the door. Having doors slammed in my face and sometimes threats issued were considered good things as martyrs for Jehovah. As a teenager, I especially hated going door-to-door, particularly in neighborhoods where I might meet classmates.

Before going door-to-door, I had to practice what to say, what scriptures to read, or any catch phrase to get the ear of the person who answered. I remember asking if the person would like to live on a Paradise earth free of pain or problems. Literature would show happy people with lions and lambs beside each other. I often wondered if the lions must have become herbivores like the lambs. But in the Jehovah's Witness religion thinking amounted to doubting, which would earn me a lecture if I dared to put a voice to my thoughts. As much as I hated corporal punishment, I sometimes would prefer it to having to stand in front of my father as he sat in his chair, forcing me to read scriptures to correct my thinking. It was easier to concede just to get past him so I could go to my bedroom where I could be alone with my thoughts.

The minutes and hours each Witness spent preaching were recorded weekly with a time sheet turned in at the Kingdom Hall. Of course, my father reviewed my time sheet, and generally I was criticized for not doing enough. He wanted me to be a pioneer, which is a missionary who spends the bulk of their time proselytizing.

One Saturday morning when I was nineteen, with only one other young woman, we were going house-to-house in a rural area. We drove up a long dirt driveway to a house secluded from view of the road. As we walked toward the house an older man sat on his front porch with a threatening look. We were scared and hurried back to the car. When I think back on the potential outcome of being raped, kidnapped or killed and maybe never being found I become angry. The elder who gave me the map knew the remote rural territory and gave no thought to sending us into harm's way.

I was so torn between two worlds, my developing real beliefs and my desire to be with the family I loved and the only people I had known.

# 4

## Money

Through the amazing ability of my mother to squeeze six cents out of every nickel, I was never hungry. Relatives and neighbors shared produce from their gardens, and in the summer and fall fruits and vegetables were canned and frozen. My father frequently stopped by farms on his way home from work to buy bulk fruits and vegetables. He told one farmer he wanted twelve dozen ears of corn and expected them to be baker's dozen. A baker's dozen is thirteen, so twelve baker's dozens meant my father brought home 156 ears of corn. As I husked the corn outside in the summer sun I was expected to count the ears and report to him the number. Sometimes there were more than 156 ears which pleased him. If there were less, I'm sure the farmer heard about it the next time my father stopped by. It was hot in the summer, but being outside husking was far better than being inside parboiling corn and cutting the kernels off the cob to freeze. The kitchen full of steam and with no air conditioning was many degrees hotter than the August heat.

The income of my father, a barber with five children, barely provided for necessities. He would often bring home guests for dinner and even invited two missionaries to live with us for a time in our modest three-bedroom home. My mother's frustration was evident when she would have to ask my father whether she could afford another bar of soap or a roll of toilet paper. My father implemented, or so he thought, a two-sheet rule for toilet paper use. Circumstances often made it difficult to obey—as was the case with many of his rulings.

My mother insisted on staying close to her siblings, despite my father's objections since they were not Jehovah's Witnesses. My maternal cousins generously handed down clothes and shoes. But as I grew to be the tallest I had the biggest feet or under-standing, I was often in need of shoes. Playing outside in the summer was not an issue, but when school was in session I desperately needed shoes. I cycled through the same clothes every few days, while I noticed classmates wearing the newest styles with an abundance of clothes to prevent them from repeating an outfit as quickly as I did. I realized that in the eyes of many students and teachers we were poor, which came as a surprise to me. We were well-fed and always had clean clothes and a warm home, so I didn't notice until my interactions at public schools.

My father believed we should only have the basics to live. "After all," he would say, "with the end of the world so near, once we enter a perfect Paradise, we will have everything." He did not believe in the need of life insurance or retirement income. We lived in the moment of today, with the hope of soon being in Paradise, and therefore no need to save money for the future. His lack of forethought proved difficult during his forced retirement due to Alzheimer's disease. He refused to take medication for his high blood pressure and ended up needing to be on dialysis for kidney failure. He expected that Armageddon and entry into Paradise where he would be a perfectly healthy man was coming soon so he would never face death. My parents did not have insurance until they were on Medicare. My mother quietly suffered many years from numerous ailments with no resources for treatment, including gall stones and breast cancer.

I worked hard to babysit for fifty cents an hour and help neighbors with yard and garden work for a few coins. I saved my money to buy clothes and shoes and Matchbox cars for my brothers and a few penny candies. My father told me to put some of the money I earned in the contribution box at the Kingdom Hall. I frequently wondered if I was selfish for wanting to spend my money on new clothes and shoes instead.

My father came up with his own ideas for me to make some money. The dirtiest, and likely the most hazardous job, was what he called cleaning copper. Two of our Witness family neighbors worked at a scrap yard. They told my father how to burn transformers to pull apart the metal in order to collect the copper inside. In a remote location the transformers were placed in a fifty gallon drum with holes punched in the sides. Gasoline was then poured over the contents of the barrel and it was lit on fire. Black smoke would pour out as the plastics melted to release the metals. My nostrils would be black from breathing the smoke and chemicals. We would wait for the fire to consume the transformers and then dump the contents out to cool. With heavy gloves I would eagerly collect the copper until I had filled my bucket. I wondered how much money I would make when my copper was weighed at the scrap yard. I imagined the many things I could buy with the few dollars it rendered. Copper was about 25 cents a pound. When my mother understood the dangers of being exposed to the heat and chemicals, she stopped me from going to collect copper. It was one of the few times I ever heard her argue with her husband. She could be a momma tiger protecting her children, knowing that in private he would chastise her for not being silent and submissive.

In my early teens my father wanted me to shine shoes at his barber shop in the summer. He enticed and badgered me with how much money I could make. His barber shop was in a truck stop, a thirty-minute drive from home. The thought of being his captive audience in the car for an hour each work day seemed incredibly unappealing. Also listening to him all day in the shop, I could imagine nothing worse, even while estimating how much I could earn and what I could buy. Once again, my mother rejected the idea of a young girl sitting at the feet of male truck drivers to shine their boots. I have the greatest respect for truck drivers and mean no disrespect. Looking back, it seemed a way for him to humble me away from my worldly ideas of wanting the fashionable clothing styles of the worldly people.

Every summer my uncle, a teacher and football coach, built a house to supplement his income. My father would help occasionally and take me along to earn a few dollars. I would try any task my father assigned me to do. When I accidentally tipped over a heavy wheelbarrow of mixed concrete, he berated me. I felt the tears burn my cheeks, as the other workers looked at me. I knew I must not cry out loud, or I would be berated even more. The cruel words of my father stung as I tried harder to please him. His disregard for my physical health, and certainly my feelings, were realized more and more as I matured. I did not see other fathers berate their children for mistakes and accidents. *Was there something wrong with me?*

Many years later the same uncle shared that my father never preached to him. It came as a shock, as it conflicted with the expectations my father had of me. It seemed to me that my father was either intimidated by people with college degrees, or he knew his beliefs could be reasonably debated.

The United States of America, and maybe other countries, recognizes churches or religious organizations as public charities or non-profits, therefore they are generally exempt from federal, state, and local income and property taxes. I wonder who gains from all the money and properties donated to the Watchtower Bible and Tract Society or the various organizations held by Jehovah's Witnesses. I never knew of them doing any charity activities such as food or clothing appeals. Members were expected to help other members or potential members out of their own pocket.

# 5

# I Pledge Allegiance

*I pledge allegiance…*

The United States of America was a mere 183 years old when I began school—an infant compared to other nations existing thousands of years on the earth. Learning the Pledge of Allegiance was one of the first things I was taught in school. Standing at attention facing the flag with one's right hand over one's heart and reciting the Pledge signaled the start of each school day. We did not just repeat the Pledge by rote though, we were taught the significance of the words.

Written in 1892, the author hoped the Pledge would be used by citizens of any country. The original read:

> "I pledge allegiance to my Flag and the Republic for which it stands, one nation, indivisible, with liberty and justice for all."

In 1923, the words, "the Flag of the United States of America" were added. To read:

> "I pledge allegiance to the Flag of the United States of America and to the Republic for which it stands, one nation, indivisible, with liberty and justice for all."

A year after my birth in 1953, in response to the Communist threat, President Eisenhower encouraged Congress to add the words "under God," and so today it reads:

> "I pledge allegiance to the Flag of the United States of America, and to the Republic for which it stands, one nation under God, indivisible, with liberty and justice for all."

My father demanded I sit at my desk during the Pledge as my classmates stood, frowning and mocking me. Later he allowed me to stand quietly in respect, until eventually he gave me a card addressed "To Whom It May Concern" with the following he would allow me to recite:

> "I have pledged my unqualified allegiance to Jehovah, the Almighty God, and to his Kingdom, for which Jesus commanded all Christians to pray. I respect the flag of the United States and acknowledge it as a symbol of freedom and justice to all. I pledge allegiance and

obedience to all the laws of the United States that are consistent with God's law, as set forth in the Bible."

Conflicted, and desiring acceptance from my peers, I stood and read aloud the words of his offering. I still have the original card he gave with 68 words compared to the 31 words of the Pledge my fellow students recited. The cadence didn't match either, so initially I stopped whenever my peers stopped speaking. I quickly abandoned the card without telling my father.

Raising a flag up the flagpole in front of the school each morning and taking it down at the end of each of day was performed by the students. I was excited when it was my turn and proudly carried the flag. I hoisted the flag up the flagpole in the morning and lowered it before school was dismissed. Sharing the exciting news of my privileged school assignment brought anger from my father that evening. He went to the school the next day demanding that I be excluded from any flag activities as well as from singing the National Anthem or God Bless America.

Expressing any embarrassment I felt at being different was harshly criticized by him. I was supposed to feel special to be one of Jehovah's Witnesses. The more I learned about this young country, the United States of America, my young, logical mind could not process why I felt special to live in America, yet had to deny any patriotism. America offered freedoms other countries denied their citizens, and I was secretly happy to be an American. It would take almost thirty years before I expressed my appreciation by casting my first vote.

Some teachers would be sensitive to my father's religious fervor, while others found ways to show their contempt. When teachers handed out assignments I was not permitted to do, some would glare at me and others would look at me with pity. Thinking back today, I wonder which teachers and students had grandfathers, fathers, brothers, and sons who fought and maybe lost their lives in wars for the United States of America. The Korean War began in 1950 and had only ended in 1953 the year I was born. World War II took place from 1939 - 1945 and World War I was from 1914 – 1918. Emotions were high.

Patriotism wasn't the only conflict at school. My father did not believe in other topics as they arose in the curriculum. When asked on a test who was the first man on the moon, I would answer, Neil Armstrong, and be graded accordingly as giving a correct answer. However, my father told me no man was or ever would be on the moon or anywhere in the heavens because they belong to Jehovah. Straddling conflicting information, after many confrontations with my father, I dealt with my fears by becoming adept at concealing potential points of disagreement. Faced with deciding what to say or to avoid saying anything at all became overwhelming. Not sharing a test result or workbook assignment he would disagree with took constant vigilance.

Living in time of tremendous advances in knowledge and technology, the divide only widened between the impact of my father's beliefs and the beliefs of the rest of the world of unbelievers or non-Jehovah's Witnesses. At the time I was in school in the 1960s the world population was about three billion. The number of Jehovah's Witnesses worldwide was likely a couple million.

# 6

## Baptism

The day of baptism was a critical date to remember in the life of a Witness. Further, according to their belief, the day of one's death was more important than the day of one's birth. Ecclesiastes 7:1, "A good name is better than precious ointment; and the day of death than the day of one's birth." I was 12 or 13 when I was pressured to be baptized, and I do not remember the date.

The pressure of family and other adults at the Kingdom Hall pushed me to get it over with to stop the incessant nagging of my father and others in the congregation. I even tried to feel some level of emotion or religious fervor, but I really didn't. I vacillated between trying to please and being true to my developing beliefs—and doubts. My father reviewed and practiced the questions and answers with me until he was satisfied I would not embarrass him. I well-knew the expected answers to the questions posed to me by an elder before baptism.

I donned my bathing suit to be submerged in the pool beneath the stage of the Kingdom Hall.

Given the enthusiasm surrounding baptism, I wondered if upon rising from the water I might feel differently. As I toweled off and changed into dry clothes, I knew nothing had changed in my thinking. The only change was the newly felt importance in the eyes of my parents and fellow members in the home congregation. I became one of the Great Crowd of chosen ones and counted as a full member. My father was proud of me... for a moment.

Congregations were expected to increase the number of hours spent preaching, the number of people attending local meetings and the number becoming baptized members. Monthly reports were sent to the Watchtower and Tract Bible Society. Circuit or traveling overseers would visit congregations to encourage or pressure members to preach more with the goal to bring in more followers, thereby saving the lives of non-Witnesses who would then survive Armageddon and be in Paradise.

The amount of contributions from the congregation to the Society was also reviewed. Members were counseled to contribute financially almost to the point of competition with other congregations in order to bolster efforts to promote the organization. Many churches teach their members to tithe, which is to give one tenth of one's annual earnings for the support of the Church and clergy. Witnesses did not tithe but were expected to give more or as much as possible. The local elders made it their business to know the finances and careers of members. And the members were expected to give everything after providing for their family's basic needs. In fact, members commonly assigned their estates of land, homes and money in their wills to the Watchtower Bible and Tract Society. After all, the firm belief was that Paradise would provide everything soon. Jehovah's Witnesses have been preaching Paradise will come soon since its inception in 1872 as an outgrowth of the International Bible Students Association in Pittsburgh Pennsylvania by its founder Charles Taze Russell.

Along with contributions of money, Witnesses volunteered innumerable hours of their time in building and maintaining Kingdom Halls. Members who were electricians, carpenters, HVAC technicians, painters and plumbers were kept in a database and called upon. Witnesses performed quick builds of most new Kingdom Halls usually within three days, similar to Amish families working together to build a barn. The foundation was completed in the weeks prior to the quick build. The goal was to finish the building and hold a meeting on the third day, a Sunday. Women were called upon to provide meals for the volunteers during the build. The motivation for quick builds was to maximize time efficiently to allow for more preaching.

Inside the Kingdom Halls was a large room with rows of chairs; platform for speakers; a bookroom to purchase Bibles, books and magazines; restrooms and a coat room. I was baptized in a small pool under the speaker's platform in the Kingdom Hall I attended. There were no stained glass windows, images, paintings or any special decoration. It was intentionally bare-boned and boring inside so that all attention would be focused on the speaker and his messages. I learned in which parts of the program I could allow my mind to wander. And remember frequently counting ceiling tiles, chairs and attendees to stifle my boredom. Sleeping was not allowed and wriggling in your seat was punishable. The chairs were not meant for comfort especially for two-hour meetings. Most buildings did not have windows, and if there were windows they remained covered.

I do recall one time a wallpaper mural of a pastoral scene was adhered to the wall behind the stage. It was nice and gave a small respite for the long hours spent in meetings. It was during meetings in my childhood that I started picking at my fingernails and rubbing the knuckles of my hands until they became calloused. My mother reprimanded me, but even today when I am stressed I still do the same.

A few years ago I was in my car with some work associates when we passed a new Kingdom Hall without windows. They knew I had been raised a Witness, so they asked what went on inside. One even asked if chickens were sacrificed. I laughed and remarked, "I wish because it would have interrupted the monotony."

The local congregation members who donated their money and time to build and maintain Kingdom Halls did not own the land or building. The Society owned the property and thereby all money if it was eventually sold. Witnesses live in wait of a time in Paradise after all the wicked are destroyed. Many discussed the mansion or home they would choose in Paradise.

Looking back as an adult, it is clear to me that baptism is frequently pushed on young adolescents without consideration or benefit of their maturity and experience. Once baptized, the fear of being judged for making mistakes and even disassociated or disfellowshipped becomes quite real.

Learning from emerging science that the brain of a child is developing well into their twenties only brings new appreciation for the way I felt as a result of the pressure to believe that I had to be baptized at such a tender age. I felt more than pressure. I was preyed upon to increase the number of

Jehovah's Witnesses. It was not an option *not* to be baptized in my adolescence.

For a while after my baptism, it was a relief to no longer be pushed about it. Sadly, my relief wouldn't last long. I would ultimately not even remember the date, but my father, the local congregation, and the International Society all knew and listed my name as a full member. And from that date forward, they scrutinized my behaviors even closer.

Baptism and remaining faithful to the beliefs of Jehovah's Witnesses to survive or be resurrected into Paradise was not the end. After Armageddon and living being in Paradise, the belief was that there will be a 1,000 year reign of Christ followed by some test to prove one's faithfulness. Even if I reached perfection in Paradise, as Adam and Eve were told to do in the Garden of Eden, I guess I could still miss the mark and sin and have my life ended. The treadmill to reach perfection, and the accompanying anxiety never end.

As a full member at baptism, there were so many beliefs and expectations I had not yet learned, as well as even more to read and absorb—and secrets. At the time I had little way of comprehending the future consequences when I would eventually stray. Baptism became a new burden, and the consequences it would have for me in the future nearly broke me.

# 7

# Disfellowshipped

When does an adolescent begin to think of their future and who they are or will become? In my teens, my wishes to attend college and become a professional were dashed by my father. He belittled me by saying, "Who do you think you are to want to be more than a Witness woman, either preaching fulltime or becoming a wife?" There was only a no-win answer.

The very thought of being a fulltime preacher or missionary repulsed me as much as walking up to doors and knocking, all the while hoping no one was home. If no one was home, I could leave a Watchtower or Awake magazine and maybe a tract for an upcoming event like the annual memorial, and I would get credit for placing literature. And if the door opened, I preferred someone to be rude and turn me away, than someone who would listen as I tried to convince them to hear the message and take the literature. I guessed some took literature in hopes I'd go away. Little did they know, any act of listening or receiving magazines or books put them on a list for mandatory return visits.

I was trained to ask the person at the door, "Would you like to live forever in perfect health on a Paradise earth?" Displaying sincerity was mandatory, but it felt like an act as I grew up. Generally, I went to doors with another Witness and watched as the other member seemed honest in their spiel. I sensed my doubts all the while, dreading being the one to speak at the next house. I learned not to express doubts to anyone for fear of being reprimanded and punished.

Sometimes a physical spanking, while painful, was short-lived compared to a sermon from my father. He sat in a comfortable chair in the living room as I was forced to stand and listen and read scriptures meant to correct my thoughts and doubts. I became a hypocrite struggling to convince myself I had to knock on the next door. The guilt trip I was on amounted to, "What if Witnesses are right and I cost the person at the door their eternal life?"

During the 1960's I saw a bumper sticker that read: *Question Authority*. Secretly I liked the thought but would never admit it. I wondered if others liked or mocked the idea. I was under strict rules that Jehovah was the only authority, and as humans, and especially for women, his ideology could never be questioned. I wanted so much to get the bumper sticker and keep it hidden. I knew there was no place in our home where it would not be found. After all, we were only allowed few belongings, and there were eyes constantly watching me.

In my early teens I met another girl at a regional assembly, and we became pen pals. I don't remember what I wrote, but it went against the party line. She reported me to her congregation elder, who then contacted an elder in the congregation I attended. Our congregational elder spoke to my father, and quite angry, my father spoke to me. Again, I was made to read scriptures and acquiesce to whatever he took issue with.

After years of rejection I found myself in my junior year of high school, barely 16, the only girl in a class of all boys. I discussed with my father, as much as he would listen, my desire to go to college and pursue a career. My teachers advised me and my father of the professional possibilities I was capable of reaching due to my aptitude and IQ scores. He refused to consider higher education. After taking as many advanced classes as I could, he forced me to go to a vocational school that year. I detested secretarial work and vacillated until the program was full. I intentionally drug my feet until the only program with openings remaining was horticulture. I wish I had acquiesced earlier to get accepted into the nursing program, as I later stumbled into the healthcare world, which became my career path.

In 1969 I became a girlfriend to a Catholic boy in my class. Being naïve, I wanted a boyfriend and wanted to believe he loved me and would always love me. I gave in to letting him have sex with me a few times. I committed the sin of fornication. I had believed he loved me and would marry me—and I could then leave my father's home. I still remember the sixteen-year-old boy asking me, "Why are you just lying there?" I had no idea what he meant, and feared that I had displeased him. I never heard of a woman having sexual pleasure. I was disoriented and numb during our encounters and felt as though I was having out of body experiences. The boy quickly tired of me, and I was devastated and heartbroken as my misguided hopes of eventual escape died.

I believed the messages my father taught me. And I accepted that it was okay for his father to molest me as a young girl because it was drilled into me that women must be submissive to men. He also taught me that I had to fight to my death if I was in danger of being raped. However, he said I could not kick or hit any man in his privates, even if he was trying to rape or kill me. Male genitals were sacred to him.

So many years later I understand, and my teenage path does not seem an enigma to me today; it seems it was inevitable.

Certainly, my desperate need to be loved and seen as an individual and not simply a cult-resource, combined with my anger at my father, and a desire to hurt him played into my decision to have a worldly, non-Witness boyfriend and eventually give in to sex. I wanted to be like the boys and girls dating at school. I didn't want to be different. To avoid such scenarios, Witness parents would often arrange gatherings such as skating, country dancing and bowling so their teenagers could meet other Witnesses.

My father was an elder and was expected to have his family under his complete control in order to provide an example of a perfect family to the congregation. A few years earlier, at a regional assembly of congregations, my father paraded his family on stage where each of us was expected to speak to our roles and commitments. I disagreed with what he expected me to say. He wanted me to say I did womanly chores such as cleaning the house, cooking, and sewing. In fact, my duties were outside as much as possible mowing, carrying firewood, and shoveling snow. I did not want his truth to become my lie. In the end I compromised, and I lied for him. A year or so later I had my Catholic boyfriend. I wonder if consciously or subconsciously I wanted to get back at my father.

In my fifties I learned the term cognitive dissonance in a psychology class. Psychology explains cognitive dissonance as what happens when a person holds contradictory beliefs and then participates in an action that goes against one or more of them. I experienced plenty of confusion and mental stress for years until I trusted my own beliefs. I am glad I did not resolve dissonance by blindly believing whatever they wanted me to believe.

As a teenage girl, and only five or six years remaining until the 1975 timeline for the destruction of all non-Witnesses, maybe I thought being with a Catholic boy, condemned by Witnesses, offered the potential for new beliefs and a different future for me. Maybe I was just a stupid girl. The brief relationship, which is a stretch to call it that, set in motion a series of events and years of turmoil for a naïve young woman— not a woman, rather an immature teenage girl. I was a *tawpie*, a Scottish term for a foolish and awkward young person. I was more than inexperienced and innocent I was brainwashed.

I confided in someone that I had a boyfriend and she immediately told my parents, who immediately questioned me. I lied, saying she made up the story. My father asked me if we ever had sex, and of course I said no. He threatened to take me to a doctor to see if I was still a virgin. I said I was, and he was relieved and eager to put the thought behind him. His only concern was how he would look to his peers, with no consideration of my state of mind.

For a couple days I thought I might be pregnant. My periods, always irregular and light, brought a time of fear and excitement. *Of course*, I reasoned, *we will get married and I will be free from the chains of my father and his religious beliefs.* I confided in my Catholic boyfriend and he took me to his priest, I was astonished by his non-judgmental and caring guidance. Walking into the Catholic Church, seen on Watchtower literature as evil, was eye opening. Maybe I could be loved and accepted. When my period started, the relationship quickly ended. I was left alone and adrift, disappointed and lost in my feelings and thoughts.

I had told the boy that my father was a conscientious objector and believed Jehovah was the only leader of the world, not any nation. The boy told me the FBI must be investigating him for treason. Fearful, I called the FBI and asked if they were investigating my father and was told no. Years later, I realize the foolishness of my action. However, my father's brother had been imprisoned as a conscientious objector during WWII.

The few, maybe handful of times I had sex as a teenager, I did not feel any physical pain or pleasure. Disoriented in my thoughts, or lack thereof, I knew it was wrong to commit fornication. My deep need to be seen as an individual, and loved, overrode my fear of the sin. The first time was so quick, it was as if it was happening to someone else and hard to believe I had even committed a sin. I remember thinking, *is this all it is? A few minutes of two bodies intertwined.*

In 1971, when I was eighteen years and one day old, I married a Witness boy in the Kingdom Hall. He was handsome and strong, and we had dated for a year. I admired his father, who was not a Witness, and dearly loved his family. His father was a happy man, especially sitting in his chair in the living room with his youngest daughter and his grandchildren on his lap.

On one of our first dates I had driven to his house in my 1966 Chevelle Malibu. On my way home, I was driving too fast around a curve on their country road and ended up on the side of a hill, my car nearly on its side. His father, as a second job, owned a used car business, junkyard and was an auto mechanic. He had a wrecker and rescued me. He was so kind. He did not berate me. He simply towed the car off the side of the hill. Remarkably, no one was hurt, and the car only had a few scratches.

Within a few months into our marriage, the elders claimed that while going door-to-door a boy in my horticulture class answered the door and reported that he had seen me having sex with the Catholic boy when I was in school. Now—over two years later and just months into my marriage -- I was questioned by the elders. I could not clearly explain why I committed fornication to their satisfaction, nor could I convince them I was repentant. The elders asked for details such as how many times and where I had sex. They asked me whether I had sex before marriage with my husband. I was as unprepared for their questioning as a sheep led to the slaughter with zero help or support. No one was allowed to be with me during the interrogations.

At almost 18 ½ years of age, three elders, men I had known all my life, sat in front of me: stern, accusing, and judging. Feeling worthless and scared and angry, I bounced between emotions at my trial. The elders said one of the boys in my horticulture class told them about my sin when a Witness knocked on his door. They stated I made the congregation look bad. The elders would deliberate and decide if I was repentant and whether or not I would be allowed to continue as a member or if I would be disfellowshipped since I was baptized. It would be weeks before the elders delivered their sentence.

It was determined that I was to be disfellowshipped. And it was required to announce my sentence to the whole congregation in attendance of a meeting at the Kingdom Hall. At the time, being disfellowshipped required a one-year mandatory sentence. I, too, was expected to attend that meeting so they could openly heap more shame upon me. The three elders were supposed to approach me throughout the year to help me repent and return to the fold. There was only one time when the youngest elder, only a few years older than me, asked me how I was doing. Anyone who couldn't see my despair and depression, would have to be blind.

My husband and I had dated for a year and never had sex before our marriage. The elders repeatedly asked me if I had had sex with my fiancé. I told them no and could tell by their faces they did not believe me. They did not ask my husband.

One of the worst moments in my life was telling my husband I had been with another man (boy) before we began dating. His righteous anger and hurt tormented me. Likewise, the elders piled on additional anger, hurt, and humiliation when they disfellowshipped me. One of my deepest regrets was the pain and anger I caused my first husband. Secretly I also wonder if I had enjoyed hurting my father.

Being disfellowshipped only caused my feelings of worthlessness to grow. In order to be reinstated, or even permitted to talk to my family, I was required to attend meetings at the Kingdom Hall. Walking into the building, I was shunned as my family and all the adults and children I had known my whole life looked away. The children, especially those I had babysat and loved, looked at me with fear, knowing they could not speak or reach out to me. If I refused to put myself through the agony of walking in and sitting through two hours of humiliation, I would never get to speak to or even touch those I loved by being reinstated.

When an older woman gave me a tender look during a meeting with a slight nod or a small smile to convey to me her love, it nearly caused me to burst into tears. I was overwhelmed with emotion. My family never spoke to me or gave me any indication of love. During this time, as decreed by my father, my name was never allowed to be spoken by my family in his home, or anywhere at any time.

My punishment, meant to shame me into repentance, slowly turned into thoughts of wanting to be dead. Were it not for my husband and his father, who was not a Witness and welcomed me into his home, I might have given in to suicide. Before my year was up, I read in the literature how a disfellowshipped person can request of the elders to be reinstated prior to the end of the one-year term. I did so and was reinstated a short time before my year was up. The hearing before the elders was brief and I was reprimanded for not attending every meeting and told I would be watched to keep the congregation clean.

While conflicted with thoughts of Armageddon and not being in Paradise as a chosen one, I wrestled with the doubts I had regarding my father's religious beliefs. When I was reinstated, I made a real effort to go door-to-door to get in good favor with my father and the elders. I was so torn between two worlds my developing, authentic beliefs which differed from those of my family; and my desire to be with my family and the people I loved.

Many years later, my father told me he destroyed my records kept in secret files at the local Kingdom Hall. I believe it was for his benefit to protect his image when new elders would see the records. He did not want it to reflect badly on him. It was never to protect me. Of course, the international office of Jehovah's Witnesses keep records on every Witness and likely still have mine even though I wrote and told them I was no longer a Witness.

It was more than neglect that impacted me, it was my father's conscientious decision to neither help me, take care of me, nor defend me. My father's lessons for me as a young girl to be subservient to her husband, and really to all men, only served to at least partially support my near fatal decision to allow my boyfriend to have sex with me. I was trained to be passive. I committed fornication.

# 8

## Forests

I love trees and the fresh air and scent of forests, except for one.

Growing up in Ohio provided many opportunities to visit forests. In the Southeastern Hocking Hills area, Hocking State Forest covers over 9000 acres with small streams cutting through rocks leaving spectacular cliffs and waterfalls. In the dry ridge areas are pines, sassafras, and black, scarlet, white and chestnut oaks trees. Hemlock, beech, black birch, red and sugar maples, yellow poplar, white ash, red oak, basswood and hickory trees grow in cool gorges and on slopes.

We dug up, dried and boiled roots from the sassafras tree to make a delicious tea. Native American tribes used sassafras as a medicine for fever, cough, and digestive problems.

Only thirty minutes from school, we took field trips to Dawes Arboretum with wonderful holly, oak, boxwood, beech and buckeyes trees. In almost 2,000 acres with over 15,000 trees and plants we collected and identified leaves for science projects.

As an adult I visited redwood forests in California, quaking aspens in Colorado, the Smoky Mountain forests and apple tree orchards in Sedona, Arizona believed to have come from the seeds of trees originally planted by Jonny Appleseed.

Sadly, I envision a different dark and sinister forest of trees bearing forbidden sins. Within the forest are fears and threats for loss of love and life.

The following is a list of forbidden sins according to the Jehovah's Witness organization. Children were required to sit with adults during all meetings, five hours a week. I heard these words from my childhood, at a time when I had no idea what most of them meant. Some sins merited disfellowshipping, becoming totally unloved and dead to everyone. Others sins merited disassociation, meaning members could speak to, but were discouraged from spending any time with the sinner. All members could be judges by refusing to associate with anyone they deemed unworthy.

I have added my comments in parentheses following some of the forbidden sins.

Forbidden to marry someone who is not a Jehovah's Witness.

Forbidden to divorce and remarry, unless the other spouse committed adultery. (The innocent spouse is expected to explain in detail the adultery to the elders to get permission to remarry.)

Forbidden to have premarital sex, which is fornication.

Forbidden to commit adultery.

Forbidden to masturbate.

Forbidden to have oral or anal sex.

Forbidden to French kiss or open mouth kiss.

Forbidden to have sexual activity with people of the same sex, homosexuality.

Forbidden to have an abortion or to use the morning after pill.

Forbidden to become a transgender or transsexual.

Forbidden for women to oppose or challenge their husbands. Women must be in total submission toward their husbands.

Forbidden to believe in the evolution theory and promote such ideas.

Forbidden to promote beliefs not taught by the organization.

Forbidden to say "lucky," cuss words, or any word similar to a cuss word, like darn or shoot.

Forbidden to challenge existing ideas of the organization, which is considered apostasy, rejecting and abandoning their beliefs. (I got lost deep into this forest early on in my life and eventually stopped challenging my father while living in his house.)

Forbidden to go to another religious service, church, or cult. (After I stopped being a Witness, I visited many different churches, even a temple and a synagogue. I never found a church "home," but enjoyed many a sermon, singing, and some very nice folks. I even attended an Emmaus Walk, a three-day course in Christianity. A pleasant experience until at the end two male pastors got in my face, similar to my experiences with the Witness elders, and told me I had to join a church.)

Forbidden to oppose the law of the organization or its representatives.

Forbidden to listen to certain types of music, movies, television shows, read certain books, play certain games, video games, or go on certain websites.

Forbidden to acquaint oneself with non-believers on a regular basis.

Forbidden to participate in sports competitions.

Forbidden to vote independently in any election. (I was 35 years old when I first voted in a presidential election.)

Forbidden to be involved in politics. (Jehovah is the only ruler.)

Forbidden to play the lottery or any gambling activity.

Forbidden to participate in any celebrations such as Halloween, Christmas, New Year's Eve, Birthdays, Mother's Day, Father's Day, national celebration days, Easter, etc.

Forbidden to receive blood transfusions, even if life is compromised.

Forbidden to eat blood or foods containing blood.

Forbidden to take vaccines and organ transplants were strictly forbidden.

Forbidden to have secondary education to college or university.

Forbidden for women to wear revealing shirts, tops, dresses, or skirts above the knee.

Forbidden to wear extremely tight pants or too baggy oversized clothing.

Forbidden for women to have privileges in the congregation such as elders or ministerial assistants. (Women could speak to women onstage for short demonstrations of how to go door-to-door or give counsel to each other as long as they looked at each other and not out at the congregation. If only women and children met together to go door-to-door, a woman was permitted to pray for the group as long as her head was covered; a tissue or handkerchief was okay to use.)

Forbidden for women to teach men the doctrine, unless there are exceptional circumstances, and then they must wear a hat as a sign of subordination to men.

Forbidden to smoke or use illegal drugs.

Unforgivable sins. (Leaving the organization and joining another church and suicide.)

I don't recall any mention of pedophilia being forbidden. In fact I've heard Witnesses now go into prisons to preach and pedophiles are eager to listen, join, and attend meetings at the Kingdom Hall upon their release.

Sexually-related sin and policing genitals seems to account for a lot of the forbidden sins. Members can report incidents to elders who were to investigate, judge, and keep the congregation clean.

Escaping the doctrines of Jehovah's Witnesses and their forest of forbidden sins was bittersweet. While I was sad for the loss of family and members I knew and loved all my life, for me the freedom and happiness surpassed the loss.

# 9

# Armageddon and Babies

My desire to have children was never in question. Babysitting my younger siblings and the children of our Witness neighbors gave me joy. Away from the critical eyes of my parents, I could be myself, confident and in charge. Parents of children I babysat for were kind and appreciated me.

Married the day after my 18th birthday in 1971 and awaiting Armageddon predicted for 1975, I was conflicted as to whether to bring a child into this dangerous pre-Armageddon world. With my own survival in question based on my mistrust of the truth and having committed fornication at 16, I wondered whether I was being selfish to start a family. I also debated internally whether I did or did not have faith in the beliefs.

Prior to the 1975 prediction, the original Jehovah's Witness leader had predicted Armageddon would transpire in 1914. When the end did not occur in 1914, a new understanding was presented, declaring a new truth that the generation living in

1914 would by no means pass away, but would live to see the end of the world. Jehovah's Witnesses have been proclaiming the impending arrival of Armageddon, the end of life for all non-Jehovah's Witnesses, and the new world order of Paradise on earth since 1879.

As a baby until I was almost thirty, I sat in the Kingdom Hall for hours every week listening to stories of fear and faith. The Kingdom Halls did not have rooms for children or nurseries. Children sat with adults hearing the atrocities of Nazi concentration camps where Jews and Jehovah's Witnesses were tortured and killed. Witnesses who would not denounce their faith despite the horrific persecutions were praised and held in high regard.

The stories I heard at the Kingdom Hall and read in the literature about Jehovah's Witnesses in Malawi were most troubling as a young woman contemplating having children. Jehovah's Witness women who refused to pledge allegiance to the dictator and denounce Jehovah had their legs tied together during childbirth resulting in the gruesome death of mother and infant. *Could I ever consider such a possibility for my baby and myself? Was I strong enough in faith to endure whatever tribulation I might face?* I assumed it was inevitable that I would one day need to protect my baby with my very life because even the thought of questioning or doubting the beliefs was considered an act of unfaithfulness.

Being faithful meant spending as many hours as possible reading the mountains of literature, attending five meetings a week as well as the regional and national assemblies, and preaching door-to-door to save others before the end. Suffering for preaching and teaching in war-torn countries and nations where leaders killed people who did not give their allegiance to the leader but to Jehovah was considered a trophy of one's faithfulness. Female Witnesses in Hitler's concentration camps were ordered to sign a paper declaring Hitler the supreme ruler, they held out declaring Jehovah as their only ruler. Being persecuted and killed for refusing to denounce the truth offered them a free pass into Paradise after their resurrection.

When Armageddon did not come in 1975, and after five years of marriage, I took a chance. Near my 23rd birthday in 1976, I became pregnant. My first son, born in 1977, brought joy beyond my wildest imagination. Loving and protecting him became my highest priority above all else. I protected him from strangers at doors I did not call on to preach, from new visitors at the Kingdom Hall, and from old members I did not trust.

Alongside the joy of the birth of my son was the heart-wrenching conflict of blood transfusion during his birth. Set to be induced on a Monday after 40 weeks of pregnancy, I went into labor the day before. My dear sister had taken me for rides in her Jeep on bumpy rural roads to encourage labor. On Sunday, I waited to go to the hospital until my contractions were regular. The first nurse to check me that afternoon said I would deliver before her shift ended. My doctor was on vacation, and I overheard his partner on-call stating he would not see me because I declined to be catheterized for a urine sample. I worked in the office of an internal medicine doctor and his wife, a nurse, who strongly advised me not to be catheterized simply to get a specimen. I was able to give a urine sample, and so I had asked not to be catheterized.

After a few hours of contractions, they suddenly stopped and the on-call doctor refused to examine me. I overheard him say to the nurses that he had seen enough of his associate's patients that weekend. The shift ended for the first nurse, who came by to wish me luck as she left. Throughout the night, nurses would have me walk the halls and stand in a warm shower. In the middle of the night, a nurse examined me and said I was having a boy. His genitals were in the birth canal. Breech birth babies come feet first; however Frank-breech babies are born bottom first, with their legs folded about the body and the umbilical cord in danger of twisting around the neck.

My obstetrician finally arrived Monday morning thinking he was there to induce me when he was informed of my situation. Immediately, I was given an IV to induce labor. He did episiotomies, incisions in the perineum, the tissue between the vaginal opening and the anus and pulled my baby from my body. My son was instantaneously taken away with a low Apgar score indicating he was in distress. It would be many hours before I would see or hold him. The doctor and nurses aggressively kneaded my abdomen to staunch the bleeding from my uterus as I passed out.

My obstetrician ordered blood transfusions, even though I had stated no blood transfusions on my hospital registration forms. Exhausted and overwhelmed, I reconsidered my decision and asked them to do whatever was necessary to keep me alive. My father marched in angry, indignant, and pious, demanding I would not receive blood and threatening legal consequences. The doctor began multiple IV fluids to replenish the fluids I had lost and canceled the order for blood transfusions. In hindsight, I understand the implications of malpractice by the doctor who refused to see me on Sunday and placed my life and the life of my son in jeopardy. I wish I had sought legal advice.

In most vaginal deliveries, the baby's head passes through the birth canal first with their soft skulls molding into an oblong shape then rest of the baby's body follows. In a Frank breech delivery, babies have their legs extended up along their body in a position where the feet are by the ears. My precious son required physical therapy, taught to me, to draw his legs down. Otherwise he was fine, and he had the most beautiful round head and face.

After breastfeeding my son for eight months, I was surprised to become pregnant again, and after the initial shock, I looked forward to another baby. On the first birthday of my son, I had a miscarriage. Three months pregnant I began bleeding while at work. Still working for the same Internal Medicine physician, he sent me to the obstetrician in the office nearby. The obstetrician was the same doctor who my mother had seen and had delivered me.

I was immediately taken to an exam room and then sent to the restroom. Suddenly, cramping and pain caused the loss of my baby. I looked at the tiny fetus in the toilet and wept inconsolably. The nurse came in and took me into an exam room beside the restroom. As the doctor entered, I heard the toilet flush, and I began screaming. My baby was going down the drain. The loss of my baby was devastating. The kind doctor gently explained, saying that some apples on a tree do not ripen, and they fall to the ground, as he cleaned afterbirth from my body. He said it was called a spontaneous abortion. I was mortified to hear the word abortion. Though it was a medical term, the words caused me even more anguish.

For months I argued with myself about the doctor's story of the apple tree. I blamed myself for doing something wrong to cause the death of what would have been my second child. Only one year from the traumatic events of my first pregnancy, my body must not have recovered. I wondered if taking a blood transfusion would have helped me heal and made me strong enough to carry another baby to term.

If I had given birth 33 years earlier, a blood transfusion would have never been an issue. Before 1944, Jehovah's Witnesses could have blood transfusions. Then in some new understanding from Jehovah to the presiding governing body at the Watchtower Bible and Tract Society, blood transfusions became a sin and grounds for expulsion or disfellowshipping. *Was this another new truth, or rather a lie and yet another way to brainwash and control believers?* To doubt the new belief was equivalent to questioning the organization and its special communications from the true God only to his chosen ones.

I believe today the governing body in the organization allows the decision of whether to accept blood transfusions and transplants on the conscience of the individual or parent. Elders may or may not take action to disfellowship the person receiving or allowing a blood transfusion. I wonder over the past years how many thousands of children and adults have died due to religious conviction not to take blood.

# 10

## It's a Tumor

"It's a tumor," the same words from two different medical doctors took my breath away.

It started out as a tiny bump under the skin near my right ear. Having dry skin, I rarely had a pimple. The bump grew from the size of a pea to the size of a walnut shell very quickly.

I was referred to an ENT surgeon who said it was a tumor of abnormal cells in the parotid gland, the largest salivary gland. He told me he had removed many in his years of practice. He said, "Surgery will take about ninety minutes, and you might have some facial paralysis as the tumor is growing rapidly around facial nerves." At only 26 years of age, having my face paralyzed was difficult to imagine.

I opted to get a second opinion from a new ENT in town. He confirmed it was a fast growing tumor and said it would take about four hours to remove and that I would have no facial paralysis. I scheduled surgery with him as soon as possible. In the 1970s patients were admitted to the hospital the day before surgery for tests and to get a good night of sleep. A nurse with a calm and confident voice gave me a relaxing massage before sleep.

The next morning the ENT came in to see me before the scheduled surgery time. He asked me if I could be pregnant, and I said I did not think so. However, one of the tests done the day before confirmed I was in fact pregnant. He explained if I went ahead with surgery, I would lose the baby. It was 1979. Things are so different now. I asked if a biopsy could be done to determine whether the tumor was benign or malignant and was told that was not an option. The concern was if the encased tumor was opened in a biopsy and had malignant cells, they could spread into my head and brain.

Canceling surgery until my baby was born carried its own set of risks. Due to how rapidly the tumor was growing it could cause nerve damage and facial paralysis. If the tumor was malignant, it could spread into other areas of my body. I asked what the chances were of the tumor being cancerous and he said 50/50. I would not lose my baby, and so I canceled the surgery. The ENT said he would monitor the growth of tumor throughout my pregnancy and suggested I wait until the baby was three months old to reschedule. I went home to my husband and nearly-two-year-old son to live and wait.

A few kind and generous folks at the Kingdom Hall purchased airfare, housing, travel, and clinic costs for me, my husband, and our son to fly to San Diego and then take a shuttle to a cancer clinic in Tijuana, Mexico. One of the ladies at the Kingdom Hall, who had previously been diagnosed with cancer, had been to the clinic several times, used their tonic, adhered to the dietary restrictions, become cancer-free, and lived well into her nineties.

Flying from Ohio to San Diego, California was an exciting experience despite the reason for going. Citizens from the United States going to the clinic were housed in the same hotel and transported by shuttle bus into Tijuana. Traveling by car and walking around the city was discouraged due to crime.

However, the Clinic was welcoming and everyone waited in a common area as they were each taken throughout the day for testing. Many patients carried x-rays and medical records for doctors to compare. Throughout the day I met many patients who had returned and shared their stories of using the treatment and being cured of different cancers. At the end of a long day each patient received their diagnosis and treatments as necessary.

A famous movie star visited the clinic, but sadly his cancer was too advanced for treatment. He was ultimately diagnosed with pleural mesothelioma, a cancer associated with asbestos exposure. His exposure came from asbestos in movie set insulation, race driver suits, and insulation in troop ships from his days in the Marines.

I was told they could not determine whether my tumor was benign or malignant, and they stated they had never treated a pregnant patient. Their usual tonic was recommended, a strict diet and a recipe book, The Good Health Cookbook, were given to me. The tonic was to be taken only during the second trimester of my pregnancy as there was no research to support possible complications. I took a black tonic daily as directed which was taken from the Hoxsley treatment.

Harry Hoxsley, N.D. was a Naturopathic Doctor who used an herbal all-natural cancer therapy based on his great-grandfather's observations and treatment. The history of the treatment is as fascinating as is his story of conflicts with the United Stated Food and Drug Administration and the American Medical Association. He was forced to move his headquarters in Texas and his seventeen clinics in major cities in the US to Tijuana, Mexico in 1964 to operate a BioMedical Clinic which continues today. There are many books and internet resources which detail patients who were cured and the efforts of the established medical community to debunk the treatment.

Dietary restrictions were no bleached white flour which is found in most breads, cereals and pastries. Unbleached, wheat and rice flours were permitted. No white sugar and salt intake should be reduced. Turbinado sugar, also known as raw organic sugar, honey and maple syrup were permitted. Turbinado sugar is a cane-based, minimally refined sugar which is brown in color with large crystals. It is considered to be healthier than both white and brown sugars because it is less processed and refined and it tastes good.

Reading labels became an obsession. I mostly ate fresh fruits and vegetables and some meats. For snacks, I went to the local Nut Shoppe, who roasted nuts daily and did not add salt for me. The local potato chip company allowed me into the conveyor room where hot chips were pulled off the belt before being salted and placed in a box.

No pork or tomato products fresh or canned were permitted. No vinegar, no carbonated beverages (pop or soda), and no alcohol were allowed. I ate mostly fresh chicken, beef, and fish, being careful not to eat any pork. Omitting tomatoes and tomato products eliminated many items from my usual diet. Ketchup, spaghetti sauce, and pizza were favorites and a bit difficult to substitute. Chocolate has refined sugar and was not allowed, so I became familiar with carob to make brownies.

The cookbook had over one hundred recipes, information about vitamins and their food sources, and practical ideas for substitutes. Sprouts, fresh fruit and vegetable juices were recommended. My favorite recipes were the oven fried chicken, white pizza, oatmeal cookies and carrot cake. Staying healthy to watch my son grow and for my unborn child made the restricted foods easier to give up.

I followed the dietary changes throughout my pregnancy and was in excellent physical health. The mental strain, however, of whether the tumor was malignant and whether I would be able to raise my babies was a nagging anxiety I tried to push away. My ENT physician monitored the size of the tumor each month. The tumor not only stopped its rapid growth, it shrank a little to the bewilderment of my doctor, who expressed skepticism of my Mexican treatment plan.

After giving birth to a healthy baby boy, I was advised to wait three months and have surgery to remove the tumor. As much as I believed the treatment at the cancer clinic in Mexico could alleviate the tumor, the cost to travel across country was unaffordable. I entered the hospital for surgery while still breastfeeding my second son. The surgery went well and caused no paralysis. The incision, the same kind used in a face lift, started in front of my right ear around the back of the ear and then down the neck. A face lift would have been more appreciated at sixty-six years of age, than when I was twenty-six years old. The tumor and most of the parotid salivary gland were removed. To this day, over forty years later, the only problem after surgery is saliva leaks from the incision every time

I eat and sometimes even if I am hungry and can only smell food.

Waiting for pathology to determine if the tumor was malignant seemed an eternity though it was only a day or two. My younger sister worked in the hospital lab and quietly shared with me that it was a mixed benign tumor. I acted surprised as my ENT surgeon shared the official results.

A benign tumor is not a malignant tumor which is cancer. As such, it does not invade nearby tissue or spread to other parts of the body the way cancer can. In most cases, the outlook with benign tumors is very good, but can be serious if they press on vital structures such as blood vessels, nerves, or vital organs such as the brain. A benign tumor can continue to grow and become malignant or cancerous. Mixed tumors result from uncontrolled, progressive multiplication of cells, serving no physiological function.

The future looked bright once more.

It would be two more years before my life would take another hard turn.

# II

## Dissolution

After ten years of marriage and the birth of two young sons, my husband notified me he was separating on a specific date in March of 1982. I couldn't process that he would really leave me and our sons. But, true to his word, on that date when I came home from work after picking up my sons, he had moved out.

Marrying at the age of eighteen and never experiencing life, he wanted a separation to explore the freedom of being single. For me, a separation did not mean dating others. For him, it did. The anguish of seeing him with young girls was beyond my imagination. The sorrow and heartache of our sons howling out each day that we came home and his truck was not in the driveway was beyond grief. I bore their sorrow and mine and the overwhelming anger and hurt expressed by my sons. My younger son, only two years old, screamed, refusing to go into the house for weeks. My older son grew quiet and reserved, suffering in silence, which continued far into his life.

At the beginning of the separation, I felt I owed him one since I had entered our marriage with the lie of virginity. I was willing to forgive and rebuild trust in our relationship, but as months rolled by, I knew I had to face my future alone. His decision brought with it enormous gut-wrenching feelings, but I suppressed my truest suffering from my sons and others.

One night after my sons were asleep, I went into the basement of the second house we had bought together. I laid myself out atop a thin carpet on a hard concrete floor, covered my face with a pillow, and screamed my own grief and defeat. In a fetal position, after weeping until I was utterly spent, I remained there long into the night. Almost forty years later, I researched a story of a murder that had occurred in that house and saw a photo of the exact same place I had laid, dying my own death of sorts.

With more mental and physical strength than I thought possible, I finally pulled myself up off the floor and climbed the stairs to face the next day. I held my sons a little too tight, and they objected to being squeezed too hard.

My husband and I had purchased our first house a few months after our first son was born. In a matter of weeks after moving in, our house was ransacked and robbed one October night. My husband worked second shift, and I had been sick that day and stayed at my parents' house for the night. After my husband's shift ended, he drove to my parents' home, and we returned to our home to find that the front door was pried open and every room and drawer and item had been touched by a thief. From that day on, I slept with a gun under my pillow.

Our nearest neighbor was an older gentleman who promised to watch out for me and would come over if I ever called. He only asked that I not shoot him. The robbery produced much fear and anger at the thought of a stranger touching my son's things. One night a few weeks after the robbery, I heard a loud noise and thought someone had crashed into our home. I awoke with a start and grabbed my gun, ready to defend my son. As I peeked out the bedroom into the living room, I saw the cast iron wood burner had fallen over and caused the noise. I'll never know what caused it to fall, but it was time to move.

The first house sold quickly, and we bought the house we were living in at the time of the dissolution. The new house was a mile from his parents, who were eager for us to live close so they could see their grandson. When we initially toured the house, the front door was padlocked by the sheriff. We knew a murder had occurred there a few years prior, so the house had sat empty with a bargain price tag. I was never afraid of ghosts, even though I was taught there is evil and there are demons.

As if the emotional and financial matters of our dissolution were not enough, here come the elders doing their duty to keep the congregation clean. The only grounds for divorce or dissolution were adultery. In order for me to ever be free to remarry, I must tell the elders my husband had committed adultery. I suggested that they ask him directly, as that was the right action to take. Whether they asked him or whether he refused to speak with them, I was never sure. I doubt they asked him. Nevertheless, they kept coming to me to find out our reasons for dissolution.

I refused to answer the elders as all the while they tried to intimidate me with threats that I must be alone forever unless I divorce for adultery. My husband told me shortly before he left that he had sex with a young women known to us. In a way I felt reprieve for my teenage sin of fornication and though hurt, I forgave him. To me, his adultery almost seemed to balance my sin of fornication before our marriage.

My father demanded I tell the elders why I was getting a divorce, which was technically called dissolution. He demanded I was not to divorce, but rather do everything possible to get him back. My husband was looking for something I could not give him, for I knew then what was lacking. During sex, I had often thought, *is this all there is?* I felt something was missing, but I would not know what it was until after our dissolution when I found a book describing the female orgasm. I was once again devastated by the abhorrent teachings of my father and the

Witnesses' with their "forest of forbidden sins" and no sex education of the female response.

I never told my father or anyone of my husband's adultery before our separation or his relationships with other women during our separation. Something within me knew the elders were merely checking a box and getting to play judges. Elders were not interested in helping restore our marriage or our faith, even though they didn't want to lose members. Even saying restore our faith over 40 years later sounds ludicrous. The elders were ignorant men without the skills to advise or reconcile us.

Men who were alcoholics and beat their wives and children were members in good standing. Men committing incest with their children and grandchildren as well as other pedophiles sat in the Kingdom Hall in good standing every week. These men were greeted and held their heads high as accepted members—the hypocrisy overlooked because they were men.

The annulment of our marriage six months after he left brought an entire new depth to the chaos of my life.

# 12

## Murder –
## "She won't bother you..."

A few years after our dissolution when I was at home with my sons, a woman called one evening. She said her name, but I did not know her. Then she said, "My daughter won't bother you. She doesn't want the house." I asked what she was talking about, and she said her daughter was out of prison and did not want the house I presently lived in. She had been the wife of the man murdered in the basement.

Though I knew there had been a murder in the house before we bought it, I knew little of the details. The man's sister lived in the house next door and was nice, but would never come into my house. The memory of her brother's murder was too painful.

Her telephone call did more to cause me to worry than to bring relief. I did not know the details of the murder, so I called the local police to advise me. The police assured me we were in no danger from the wife, who had been convicted along with her girlfriend who was still in prison. Living alone, I had felt relatively safe in the small village of less than 3,000 people. I no longer had a gun after the dissolution as I was more afraid my sons might find it.

Decades later, upon the writing of this book, I called the County Court House where the trial was held and asked to review the records. Since the murder and trial occurred over forty years ago, I was told they would have to pull the records from storage. I obtained copies of the records, and I was in for a shock when I saw a photo of the dead body taken in the house where I had lived for ten years.

The case began on a cold morning four days into a new year with a 45-year-old wife going to the house of a neighbor, her sister-in-law, stating intruders had broken in and shot her husband. Paramedics were called, but the husband was dead from a gaping shotgun wound in the chest. The hysterical wife was taken to the hospital with bruises and abrasions on her face, head, wrists, and ankles. She told the sheriff that she and her husband were awakened as several people came into their bedroom. She said she was taken into the basement, knocked unconscious, and wired to a chair for hours before she freed herself.

The husband has been brutally beaten on the forehead and there were bloodstains throughout the house. Crime technicians dusted for fingerprints, photographed scenes, and collected evidence. The house was ransacked, but nothing appeared to be taken except the wife's car, which was missing, and the victim's shotgun. The theory was that the husband was killed with his own shotgun as he tried to reach for it in self-defense.

Over the next few days more details became available, and the wife's car was found in an airport parking lot over an hour from the home. Police reviewed the list of names for airline reservations. They were interested in finding a 27-year-old woman who had been a constant companion to the wife for months. Observers at a party noted the two women kissing and fondling each other. A waitress observed the two women in serious hushed conversation with a man on another occasion.

Police wondered if the lesbian love affair was important enough to kill off the husband. Police learned the wife had convinced her husband to take out a large insurance policy, and the wife had stashed $10,000 in a local bank. The younger woman was traced to Florida from calls the wife was making to her, and she was then taken into custody. A murder warrant was issued for her, and upon searching her trailer park home, the shotgun used to kill the husband was recovered.

When she returned to Ohio, the young woman initially stated the wife was not involved. Later though, she described how the two had plotted his death for over four months. She stated they had approached a man to hire as a hit man and considered various methods of murder. She agreed to turn state's evidence since the wife had squealed on her by telling authorities where to find her in Florida. The prosecution agreed to drop the death penalty, and the young woman admitted to being the one who fired the shotgun. She described how the wife assisted her by showing her where the shotgun was kept, helping her with the phony robbery cover-up, giving her money and the keys to her car to flee. With her pleading guilty, the judge gave her a sentence of life in prison without need of a trial.

The wife told authorities the same story, admitting that the two women were lovers, and she was charged with murder. While selecting a jury, each prospective juror was asked if they would be influenced by the fact the two women were lesbian lovers. Those selected said they would judge the case on the merits of evidence, not the women's sexual lifestyle. During the trial, the wife was asked why she didn't just get a divorce and she stated she feared her husband would get the house and everything else. Despite telling numerous different stories and claiming not to remember details, her memory improved quickly as facts became clearer. For example, it was found that the basement window had been broken from the inside out, revealed by the placement of the glass particles.

As the trial went on, the confessed murderess stated the victim was talking to a lawyer about a divorce prior to his murder. The two women offered $1,500 to a man to run him down in a parking lot and make it look like an accident. When the prospective hit man showed no interest in the plan, the two women made a new plan of their own. The man testified at the trial that he was offered money, but that he never intended to do the job.

One night, after bowling and having drinks in a bar, the two women went home. The younger woman hit the victim in the head with a ball peen hammer three or four times while he slept in bed. The wife held a claw hammer and was supposed to finish the job. Thinking he was dead, the women went into the kitchen for a beer. To their surprise the victim appeared in the kitchen, standing and "bleeding real bad" from a gash over his eye. The wife had loaded the shotgun in case it was needed, and the younger woman shot him.

The younger woman then hogtied the wife and hit her a few times to make it look like a burglar had beaten her. The younger woman said it was understood the wife would "...provide me room and board and things." The wife gave her getaway money from her dead husband's wallet and from other places where cash was hidden in the house as well as the keys to her car. She drove to the airport, where she abandoned the car and took a cab into town to take a bus to Florida.

The wife spun different stories of being afraid the woman would harm her, and she didn't know anything about a plan to murder. She failed a lie detector test. Under cross-examination, she admitted she and her husband had discussed divorce and agreed to "…stick it out for one year." When asked if the year was up at the time of his death the wife said, "Yes, almost to the day."

After deliberating for seven hours the jury of 10 women and two men found the wife guilty of aggravated murder and murder for hire. The judge could have given her the death penalty, but instead sentenced her to life in prison. Only ten years later a parole board recommended the wife's sentence be commuted to a term of ten years, and she was released.

"True Detective" magazine covered the story of the murder, writing over nine pages of the convoluted tale. The headline read, "Hell Hath No Fury like a Greedy Lesbian!"

I am glad I did not know the details of the murder when I was living in the house. If I had known the wife was so deceptive and such a liar, I would have doubted what her mother told me even more. The house had been so important to the wife as a home for her and her lesbian lover that she killed for it. After only ten years in prison, should I have believed she did not want the house and would not bother me?

The worst shock was seeing the photo of the dead husband. Knowing I had lain in the same place where he died gave me chills. I felt like dying when my marriage ended. Divorce is like a death. It is the death of a promise and the murder of a future life planned for a family.

# 13

## New Beginnings

My first ever birthday party was a new beginning and given to me by coworkers on my 30th birthday. They gave me a cake with candles, decorated the lunch room with balloons and party favors made for a young child, and brought me fun presents. I was surprised and awkward as they sang Happy Birthday to me. For the first time in my life I blew out candles and made a wish. It was a year after my marriage ended and I wished for more new beginnings.

I moved to a new city, a suburb of Columbus Ohio, in 1987 at the age of almost 35, with two sons in elementary school. I felt the way I presumed an 18-year-old feels when leaving home for college. I was free—free of critical eyes and toxic relationships. I had freedom.

I rented a small second-story two-bedroom apartment for us to live in, and I rented out my house to a teacher who bought it after her one-year lease expired. I thought I couldn't truly make a fresh start until my house sold. I was wrong. I took a leap of faith in myself and found a job, the best public schools for my sons, and a community of people I was eager to get to know.

I felt safe and like the world was my oyster. The oyster had been hard to open, but was so good once I moved. Living in the big city in the 1990s was a time when there were a plethora of jokes bashing men. Before that, there had been plenty of dumb blonde jokes. Comedians were good at telling funny jokes to bash men and I enjoyed repeating them at work and at home. One day my youngest son, not yet a teen, asked me why I enjoyed the jokes, and I told him that I found them funny.

He looked at me seriously and said, "Mom, I'm a man."

I never told another joke bashing men.

Growing up, my places of safety were school, libraries, and the homes of my favorite (non-Witness) aunts and uncles. My junior high school was beside the county library. I frequented it as much as I could as it was my haven of knowledge and place of protection. My mother's little brother was a former teacher, high school football coach, house contractor—and not a Witness. Not long ago, he explained to me, his now 66-year-old niece, the power of a parents' influence. He shared that in elementary school, a child is influenced 90% of the time by parents, in middle school 50% of the time, and in high school only 10% of the time, as a child continues to increase his or her interactions with teachers and friends at school. The impact of the beliefs forced upon me by my father only banged up against my personal logic and common sense. There had been no middle ground.

I questioned the beliefs of my father which did not make sense to me so many times until I just gave up. My new and judicious friend, Joan, who I enjoy lunches with now, said her father used the term horse sense—like common sense, when something heard doesn't seem right, it's time to ask questions. Horse sense includes questioning what the eyes see and the ears hear.

My parents and siblings were splintered between Witnesses and non-Witnesses. I chose to move, and in so doing, knew I would miss the few activities with family I might have had. Even though I no longer went to the Kingdom Hall or claimed to be a Witness and I wasn't officially disfellowshipped so my family could speak to me as long as we never mentioned Jehovah or any of the beliefs. I now so appreciate my younger sister and youngest brother who are in my life and are no longer Witnesses. The decision to move and find new beginnings was so right for me. I made new friends. People liked or didn't like me for me.

The move was difficult in some ways for my sons as the school lessons were more advanced compared to the school we left in a rural Appalachian county. I also didn't realize the differences of societies in rural and metropolitan communities. We lived in an affluent community but in an area called the golden ghetto. Most families were rich and considered natives and some didn't like us because we were outsiders. Fortunately there were some native families and some outsiders who welcomed us.

My sons were tall for their ages and good athletes. In elementary school I had to show the birth certificates of my sons when questioned about their eligibility to play on teams. My oldest son was given the nickname Downtown Kurtis at his first game because he hit the baseball so far it seemed it could go all the way into downtown Columbus. He later became a top player on the rugby team in high school. My younger son played baseball, basketball and soccer and earned recognition for his skills and hard work. Some parents congratulated me, while others glared when my sons made a great play or were named MVP. I loved attending their games and sitting with parents who welcomed me. My challenge was often trying to be in two places at the same when they were both playing. Parents would fill me in on the plays I missed as I traveled between games.

My first friend lived a couple buildings from my apartment with a son the same age as my younger son. She was so accepting, caring and fun. She invited us to her church. We attended occasionally and I enjoyed some of the sermons, the welcome as we were greeted by those sitting nearby, the singing and the beauty of the church. My sons attended their summer camp for many years which is located in the beautiful hills of southeastern Ohio. The camp is known for lots of fun and games, relaxing times of reflection, and a community of friends and counselors who loved them for the unique people they were. Writing the last sentence I have tears in my eyes for the happiness my sons enjoyed at camp and a few for the missed opportunities for myself as a child.

One of the difficulties of the move for my sons was being an hour away from family. There was a time when I told my father I would not allow my sons to visit if he continued to tell them I was condemning them to death and from entering eternal life in Paradise. My sons were two and four when I stopped attending meetings at the Kingdom Hall, and so they did not understand his beliefs. When I started celebrating Christmas with my boys, my father told them that I was a bad mother who did not love them.

When my oldest son was about ten years old, he was especially hurt and confused by his grandfather's cruel and unkind words and judgements.

My father saw a level of anger from me he had never seen, and he heard many swearwords when I told him I would discontinue from the few visits we had at his home if he did not stop saying upsetting things to my sons. After some time had passed, I asked my sons if he was still saying cruel things, and they said he had told them not to say anything to me when he did sermonize to them. I restated to him the seriousness of him never seeing his grandsons again, even though I knew my mother would be hurt.

He seemed to stop sermonizing, but still made an occasional negative comment. My sons loved their grandmother, and she protected them during visits. If they stayed for a rare weekend visit, I would not let them go to the Kingdom Hall on Sunday. My father insisted my mother and the boys listen to the live program, which I think was over the phone. Mom played cards or board games with them while the meeting played quietly in the background. If he questioned them about the content, they learned to divert the conversation.

As a single mother I shared many joys, struggles, and complexities raising my sons and searched for help from books, friends, psychologists, and teachers. In 1982 we created the following house rules when my sons were 13 and 15 years old. These rules were written before cell phones when we only had one landline telephone at home:

1.  PHONES
    Mom's calls are priority. When a call for Mom comes in on call-waiting, give the call to Mom. If Mom is not home, take a message with name of person, time of call, phone number, and any message.

2.  FRIENDS

    Can visit at home ONLY when Mom is here.

    Mom must know the friend's full name, parents' names and telephone number.

    Activities such as game, movie, walk, dinner permitted.

3.  CLEANING/LAUNDRY
    Each person is responsible for their own laundry. When clothes are washed, they must be dried and put away the same day.
    Beds are to be made after waking every morning, clothes picked up, and room left neat
    Dirty dishes go in the dishwasher

4.  HOMEWORK

Must be finished every night before TV, etc.

Any homework not finished on time will result in no privileges on weekend.

Privileges include using the phone, being with friends, seeing movies, etc.

Today I can look back with laughter at the list.

My daughters-in-law have thanked me for teaching their husbands to do laundry, clean and cook.

Raising sons as a single woman was hard. Their teen years sometimes brought me to my knees as I faced the most difficult choices. My unconditional love for my sons and wanting them to have a better life and freedoms than I had has always been at the center of my motives.

About twenty years after my move, I worked with a young lady who became my cherished chosen daughter. I recognized something about her that reminded me of myself. She shared with me that her place of safety as a child was her church. She said, "I skipped down the street to church on Sunday and throughout the week." For her, church was a sanctuary. She was safely away from the chaos created by her parents at home. Her mother could be wildly animated and fun to play with or withdrawn and sad. Her father was a frightening presence of impending dark deeds upon his children, deeds kept secret for decades while splitting memories and relationships amongst the children for even longer.

Sometimes when speaking honestly, words may be heard or words may fall on deaf ears not ready to hear them. Few are ready to accept the realities of childhoods filled with unspoken or not remembered abuses. Sometimes secrets kept in the deepest recesses of the mind and body can become too painful to even peek into. Feelings hang like dark clouds, preventing light from reaching the facts, long ago buried.

# 14

## Laura and Laura

My first Laura...

After moving to the big city I searched for a psychologist, knowing I needed help. The first male psychologist I met with invited me to a party, which seemed inappropriate. The second person was young and seemed distracted. The third psychologist, Dr. Laura, was just right. She was a professional woman about my age. After a brief explanation of my reason for seeing her, she said I needed to be deprogrammed. I am forever grateful for the help she provided.

I was surprised how weekly one hour visits with her began to transform my thoughts and feelings. I became more confident and less plagued with negative reactions to the news. Witnesses acquaint any news of turmoil in the world to the upcoming Great Tribulation and war of Armageddon. There was even a news story of birds increasing in numbers. It was interpreted to mean more birds would be needed to eat the carrion from billions of humans who died at Armageddon. The programming or brainwashing was difficult to turn off, but I gradually gained more and more freedom from it. Unwelcome thoughts may pop up even today, but they are quickly dispelled.

At one visit I tried to explain to Dr. Laura that I struggled with what to believe and what to teach my sons. Offhandedly she said, "You are a Christian, aren't you?" I hesitated, but felt like I had to answer *yes* based on the way she posed the question. In my mind at the time I did not believe I was a Christian. I did not know what being a Christian meant. Every day was a challenge and an adventure.

Jehovah's Witnesses are a cult, mostly centered around Jehovah being the one true God and Christ Jesus, his son, seemed to play a minor role. As I searched religions I found that being Christian can mean many different beliefs and interpretations of the Bible. Christianity is based on the life and teachings of Jesus of Nazareth. Christians believe Jesus is the Christ, whose coming as the Messiah was prophesied in the Old Testament with his life recorded in the New Testament. My basic understanding is that a Christian is a person who must accept they are a sinner and need Jesus to save them. As one of Jehovah's Witnesses, I never felt saved and do not believe in this today. I do, however, appreciate the teachings written of Jesus to love one another.

Catholic, Orthodox, Protestant, Baptist, Lutheran, Methodist, Mormons, Jehovah's Witnesses and a myriad of other churches are listed as Christian. One internet site states there are 37 million churches in the world with 34,000 Christian denominations.

I asked my father, "Do you believe in unconditional love?"

His answer was, "No, my love is based on whether you go to the Kingdom Hall, preach door-to-door, and follow all the laws of Jehovah." After many years and tears, I knew I never had, nor would ever have, his unconditional love. It is such a heartbreaking life to never have a father's unconditional love. I heard somewhere that our relationship with our earthly father affects our relationship with a heavenly father.

The Bible speaks of love many times, such as, 1 John 4:16: "God is love..." I do not need a symbol, such as the cross, or an idol or name for God other than maybe Love. I am content in my belief. I do my best to love every day and apologize for all the times I fail. I taught my children to love, to be kind, and to have good morals. All my children forever have my unconditional love.

My next Laura...

Dr. Laura Schlessinger has had an enormous positive impact on my life as a person, a woman, a wife, a mother, a daughter, a sister, and a friend. In the many years I have listened to her radio and Sirius programs, she has taught me lessons beyond anything I ever dreamed possible. Her abilities to resolve problems with adults and children inspire and motivate me.

I think I was in my thirties when I first heard her on the radio. For Christmas in 1995 a friend gave me her book, Ten Stupid Things Women Do to Mess up Their Lives. I'd rather not say how many of the ten stupid things I've done, and I only wish I had the book in my teens. Her book has a warning on the back cover, "This book is not for the faint of heart or psyche! If you really want to change, it can jump-start your journey to self-worth."

Self-worth was missing throughout much of my childhood, and much of my life, as I looked to my father and his beliefs for my worth, self-esteem, self-respect, and self-confidence that I needed to give to myself by way of my own choices and actions. What a concept. I also appreciated and learned much from her book, *Bad Childhood, Good Life: How to Blossom and Thrive in Spite of an Unhappy Childhood.*

I insisted my sons read her book, Ten Stupid Things Boys Do to Mess up Their Lives.

When I re-married in my late forties I often reached for her books. I had been divorced for many years and never lived with anyone other than my children. I was very independent, making my own decisions and not answering to anyone. The Proper Care and Feeding of Husbands and The Proper Care and Feeding of Marriage saved me many times as I navigated the complexities of marriage.

Dr. Laura's straight-forward direct words are what I needed. I agree with her most of the time. I remember a caller asking about a situation with relatives who were Jehovah's Witnesses. She answered in her reasonable and logical way. Unfortunately, reason and logic do not work for them. They will kick family to the curb and not look back.

I burned all the literature I had from Jehovah's Witnesses before I moved to the big city. That felt so good! I have since read thousands of fiction and non-fiction books and want to read thousands more. I can now understand nuances of situations and emotions unknown to me for much of my life. My editor asked me to expound on feelings in childhood and school. This was extremely difficult as I was so conditioned and programmed to be stoic and passive.

I am so thankful to my two Laura's for deprogramming me and opening my mind to embrace new thoughts and beliefs.

# 15

## Phil and Phil

In my thirties, my new friends told me about an opportunity for personal growth. The enthusiasm of my friends convinced me a self-improvement program was worth far more than the costs to travel and attend. Looking to expand knowledge of myself I was eager to be part of the group. YOU seminars, out of Wichita Falls, Texas, enrolled one hundred attendees from all over the United States for weekend retreats.

Flying into Dallas/Fort Worth airport and then taking a puddle jumper plane to Wichita Falls, we were greeted with applause as the happy volunteers stood to usher the attendees into the hotel ballroom. Loud rock and roll music played, and I nervously wondered what I had gotten myself into this time. On my application I had described myself as a Rigid Robot, and had forgotten all about it when I was given a name tag with those same words upon registration. I was appalled at the term and anxious to rid myself of it.

Reviewing the agenda for the next two and half days, followed by introductions, commenced the evening. A lesson began on hugging. An almost equal number of men and women moved along a line from person to person to embrace for a long hug. Each hug seemed an eternity compared to the usual quick hugs most people give. Men seemed uncomfortable hugging other men, and I was wary of some of the male strangers. The ability to truly and fully hug another person began to open my mind and heart engendering trust with time.

I was moved from elation to despair to elation to understanding as personal and often painful stories were shared in the group. Attendees shared intimate experiences with the whole group and in dyads, groups of two. In one exercise, the leader, Phil, read an emotional story of a fictional epidemic. Each attendee was to imagine that they held the only ten doses of medication to save ten lives. We were asked to decide who we would give the life-saving medication to. I listed the ten most important people in my life, my sons being first.

Standing face to face with Phil, he questioned, "How is that working for you?" in what I considered a deriding tone of voice. It did not occur to me to give one of the ten doses to myself. I was raised to put others first and believe that I was unimportant. The idea of putting myself first, much like putting the oxygen mask on first in a plane to enable yourself to then help others, never even occurred to me. I was a rigid robot programmed and brainwashed to serve others.

Phil's question left me reeling with uncertainty, frustration, and embarrassment for fear I had given a wrong answer, and unsure why I didn't know the right one. I was perplexed and stuttered to explain. A teammate spoke up and was quickly rebuked as Phil moved on to another attendee. The lesson was difficult before it became enlightening.

Each attendee was given a song. The song chosen for me was "In Your Eyes," a single by American R&B singer George Benson in the mid-eighties. The words reached inside this robot:

"I think I finally know you

I can see beyond your smile

I think that I can show you

That what we have is still worthwhile

Don't you know that love's just like the thread

That keeps unraveling but then

It ties us back together in the end

In your eyes, I can see my dream's reflections

In your eyes, found the answers to my questions

In your eyes, I can see the reasons why our love's alive

In your eyes, we're drifting safely back to shore

And I think I've finally learned to love you more


You warned me that life changes

That no one really knows

Whether time would make us strangers

Or whether time would make us grow

Even though the winds of time will change

In a world where nothing stays the same

Through it all our love will still remain


In your eyes, I can see the reasons why our love's alive

In your eyes, we're drifting safely back to shore

And I think I've finally learned to love you more"

Robots don't feel and can't express human emotions. I must have called myself a rigid robot on the application because I knew deep down that I needed to feel my long buried emotions and express real feelings. In a darkened room, I finally gave words to my anger.

A song played for our group was, "What's The Name of the Game," a 1977 song by Swedish pop group ABBA. These lyrics would continue to reveal new meanings to me over the days and years ahead:

> "I've seen you twice, in a short time
>
> Only a week since we started
>
> It seems to me, for every time
>
> I'm getting more open-hearted
>
> I was an impossible case
>
> No one ever could reach me
>
> But I think I can see in your face
>
> There's a lot you can teach me
>
> So I wanna know.

What's the name of the game?

Does it mean anything to you?

What's the name of the game?

Can you feel it the way I do?

Tell me please, 'cause I have to know

I'm a bashful child, beginning to grow


And you make me talk

And you make me feel

And you make me show

What I'm trying to conceal

If I trust in you, would you let me down?

Would you laugh at me, if I said I care for you?

Could you feel the same way too?

I wanna know…


The name of the game


I have no friends, no one to see

And I am never invited

Now I am here, talking to you

No wonder I get excited


Your smile and the sound of your voice

And the way you see through me

Got a feeling, you give me no choice

But it means a lot to me

So I wanna know


What's the name of the game?

(Your smile and the sound of your voice)

Does it mean anything to you?

(Got a feeling you give me no choice)

But it means a lot, what's the name of the game?

(Your smile and the sound of your voice)

Can you feel it the way I do?

Tell me please, 'cause I have to know

I'm a bashful child, beginning to grow


And you make me talk

And you make me feel

And you make me show

What I'm trying to conceal

If I trust in you, would you let me down?

Would you laugh at me, if I said I care for you?

Could you feel the same way too?

I wanna know…

Oh yes I wanna know…"


Another song I related to and heard with new appreciation are the lyrics of "New Attitude" performed by Patti LaBelle and released in December 1984. It was one of the theme songs used by Dr. Laura Schlessinger.

Running hot

Running cold

I was running into overload

That was extreme


I took it so high, so low, so long

There was nowhere to go like a bad dream

Somehow that wires uncrossed

The table were turned

Never knew I had such a lesson to learn


I'm feeling good from my hat to my shoe

know where I am going and I know what to do

I've tidied up my point of view

I've got a new attitude

I'm in control

My worries are few

'Cause I got love like I never knew

Ooo, ooo, ooo, ooo

I've got a new attitude


I am wearing a new dress, a new hat

Brand new ideas

As a matter of fact

I've changed for good


Must have been the cold nights, new moon

Night changes

Or forget your love for just being like I should.


My breakthrough was: "I am a *real* strong woman." The emphasis is on the word *real*. Real, meaning a genuine and authentic person true to myself. Strong, meaning I have the ability to stand up for my beliefs, not the beliefs of my father, or of other Witnesses, even at the cost of losing loved ones. It took days and hours of intense, honest work to understand the depth of which I hid feelings. I was no longer a rigid robot. I was euphoric on the flight home, excited to truly believe in myself.

Phil was Dr. Phil McGraw who created the self-empowerment trainings in 1985. Oprah first met Phil in 1996, when she was on trial with the beef industry in Texas. Oprah hired Dr. Phil to assist and counsel her and learned about his straight-forward approach to life coaching. She then gave him a talk show.

Now called Pathways, for over 30 years, through these three-day intensive weekend retreats, thousands of people have successfully realized their potential in living their lives, improving their family relationships, and discovering their inner power. Pathway's belief is that each person deserves a chance to live a life by design, rather than default. Any circumstance can be overcome, all wounds can be healed, and no two people's paths are the same. The experiential trainings are uniquely individualized. Each trainee identifies what they want and how they can make positive changes to achieve it. You can learn more online at Pathways Core Training Texas:

My other Phil ---

Love walked into our home.

A tired, old Rottweiler mix walked down the street on a hot summer day. My son called to the dog to offer him a bowl of cool water. The dog drank and moved into the shade to sit with him. The tag said his name was Phil, and I called the phone number on the dog tag. The owner, Matt, interrogated me, as he was concerned about why his dog was in my neighborhood.

Phil fit right in with us: my two sons, me, our hyperactive dog Katie, and our cat who ruled us all without claws. My sons and I agreed we would like to keep Phil. Matt questioned me about our motives and visited with me as one of my sons took Phil to a park. Matt did not want to have Phil see him as it would upset both of them. He sat in his car across the street and watched as my son brought Phil back. With tears in his eyes, Matt nodded his approval for Phil to be with us.

Years ago, when Matt, was a teenager, hefound an abandoned puppy alone on a street. He took the puppy home, and named him Phil, and Phil remained with him throughout high school, college, and marriage. After the birth of his first child, Phil, now 12 years old, did not want anything to do with the baby and would growl. Matt's veterinarian said that to be on the safe side, Phil should not have any contact with the baby. Matt was devastated. For a while the vet kenneled Phil, as they searched for a new forever home. They had found a home for Phil, and so Matt was shocked when I called. Phil was supposed to be in a neighborhood east of my home. He was walking past my home toward Matt's home to the west of us.

My sons, teenagers at the time, loved Phil and walked and played with him. Phil became my close friend and travel companion. Just the two of us traveled in my car from Ohio to Arizona and Colorado staying at campgrounds with small cabins. With Phil, I was safe. I sent postcards of Phil to his first family sitting at the top of the Grand Canyon and standing on a corner in Winslow, Arizona.

We hiked the trails and streams in the Red Rock Canyon of Sedona Arizona. Walking across an especially rocky stream, I stumbled and Phil went ahead of me and brought back a long stick I used to steady myself. On the other side of the stream was a rock about two feet high with the center scooped out like the back of a chair. I curled up inside the warmth of the rock with Phil at my feet and we took a nap in the sunlight. After our nap we hiked up a small hill and made a round medicine wheel with spokes made of rocks. When I finished, Phil walked into the wheel and sat within a spoke. He was the best remedy for my loneliness and a best loyal friend.

A year after Phil joined our family, and my youngest son graduated high school, we all moved from Ohio to Durango, Colorado. I drove a large moving truck and towed my car, and each of my sons drove their cars with our menagerie of pets. Within six months, my sons moved back to Ohio. A year later I moved back as well, and sadly Phil died within a few days.

When Phil died my intuition told me to wait awhile to call his original owner. I was very emotional at his loss. Months later when I finally called Phil's original owner, he shared that his father had also died—near the time Phil died. He appreciated that I had waited to deliver the news, as he was very emotional at the loss of his father. He said he could now envision his father and Phil playing together.

# 16

---

# Colorado

Many times I have wondered if someone or something in the universe watches over me. Driving from Ohio to Colorado in July that year could have gone terribly wrong, but it didn't. Approximately 1,400 miles from our home in Ohio, we drove across Wolf Creek Pass at an elevation of 10,857 feet. We were an eclectic caravan: me, in the largest moving truck I could drive, towing my car, and my sons in their cars with our two dogs, a cat, and a large fish tank.

Wolf Creek Pass was once a two-lane road winding through the San Juan Mountains between South Fork, Colorado, and Pagosa Springs. It has since been expanded into a multi-lane highway, greatly increasing the traffic capacity and making it more traversable in bad weather. The pass provides the easiest access to southwest Colorado from the rest of the state, as all remaining overland routes require lengthy detours through New Mexico or over Lizard Head Pass, near Telluride, or the intimidating Red Mountain Pass, a two-lane road winding along sheer cliffs from Ouray to Silverton.

Wolf Creek Pass is a high mountain pass on the Continental Divide of Colorado. It is the route through which U.S. Highway 160 passes from the San Luis Valley into southwest Colorado on its way to New Mexico and Arizona. The pass is significantly steep on either side (6.8% maximum grade) and can be more dangerous in winter. There are two runaway truck ramps on the westbound side for truckers who may lose their brakes.

As I passed the last runaway truck ramp, I could smell my burning brakes as I eased around the last switchbacks in the pass. I could see the cliff ahead and prayed my sons would not see me die. Soon my foot was to the floor, and I shifted to the lowest gear. Following behind, my sons watched chunks of the brakes flying off the wheels of the moving truck. After the last curve, the road straightened, and I pulled the emergency brake, remarkably coming to a stop.

Wolf Creek Pass is the inspiration of a C. W. McCall song with words I can relate to:

"Me an' Earl was haulin' chickens on a flatbed out of Wiggins, and we'd spent all night on the uphill side of thirty-seven miles of hell called Wolf Creek Pass, which is up on the Great Divide.

Well, Earl put down his bottle, mashed his foot down on the throttle, and then a couple'a boobs with a thousand cubes in a nineteen-forty-eight Peterbilt screamed to life. We woke up the chickens.

Well, we roared up offa that shoulder sprayin' pine cones, rocks, and boulders, and put four hundred head of them Rhode Island reds and a couple a' burnt-out roosters on the line. Look out below; 'cause here we go!

Well, we commenced to truckin' and them hens commenced to cluckin' and then Earl took out a match and scratched his pants and lit up the unused half of a dollar cigar and took a puff. Says "My, ain't this purdy up here."

I says, "Earl, this hill can spill us. You better slow down or you gonna kill us. Just make one mistake and it's the Pearly Gates for them eighty-five crates a' USDA-approved cluckers. You wanna hit second?"

Well, Earl grabbed on the shifter and he stabbed her into fifth gear and then the chromium-plated, fully-illuminated genuine accessory shift knob come right off in his hand. I says, "You wanna screw that thing back on, Earl?"

He was tryin' to thread it on there when the fire fell off a' his cigar and dropped on down, sorta rolled around, and then lit in the cuff of Earl's pants and burned a hole in his sock. Yeah, sorta set him right on fire.

I looked on outta the window and I started countin' phone poles, goin' by at the rate of four to the seventh power. Well I put two and two together, and added twelve and carried five; come up with twenty-two thousand telephone poles an hour.

I looked at Earl and his eyes was wide, his lip was curled, and his leg was fried. And his hand was froze to the wheel like a tongue to a sled in the middle of a blizzard. I says, "Earl, I'm not the type to complain; but the time has come for me to explain that if you don't apply some brake real soon, they're gonna have to pick us up with a stick and a spoon."

Well, Earl rared back, and cocked his leg, stepped as down as hard as he could on the brake, and the pedal went clear to the floor and stayed there, right there on the floor. He said it was sorta like steppin' on a plum.

Well, from there on down it just wasn't real purdy: it was hairpin county and switchback city. One of 'em looked like a can full'a worms; another one looked like malaria germs. Right in the middle of the whole damn show was a real nice tunnel, now wouldn't you know?

Sign says clearance to the twelve-foot line, but the chickens was stacked to thirteen-nine. Well we shot that tunnel at a hundred-and-ten, like gas through a funnel and eggs through a hen, and we took that top row of chickens off slicker than scum off a Louisiana swamp. Went down and around and around and down 'til we run outta ground at the edge of town. Bashed into the side of the feed store... In downtown Pagosa Springs.

Wolf Creek Pass, way up on the Great Divide

Truckin' on down the other side"

The song has a fun jingle and chorus and I can laugh now that I survived. The moving truck was towed over sixty miles to our new home. We only lost the fish.

*What was I thinking?* Raising my two sons alone from their ages of four and two, I dangled a carrot before me. I was a child when I became fascinated with a faded calendar picture of the Rocky Mountains on my Granny's wall. I told her I wanted to go there and maybe live there someday. Driving to Colorado for vacations, sometimes alone, was my favorite destination. Money was always a consideration, so I stayed in small Kampgrounds of America cabins, ate a lot of Wendy's, and drank many of their iced teas. On other trips I traveled north of Interstate Route 70 from Denver to Boulder and Estes Park with the Rocky Mountain National Forest and south to Durango where I fell in love.

After my youngest graduated from high school and was recruited to play baseball at a college in Arizona, I considered moving to Phoenix for a short time and interviewed for jobs. My heart was in the mountains of Colorado though, and I had promised myself to return to my dream.

Cashing in my retirement money, I flew to Durango and found a condo to rent. The condo was the middle unit of three, in an old Boy Scout Camp lodge. It was at an elevation of almost 8,000 feet with the Florida River running behind it. I kept my bedroom window open to hear the music of the river year round. I breathe better in crisp mountain air. Some folks suffer from acute mountain sickness, also known as altitude sickness or high altitude pulmonary edema. It generally occurs at about 8,000 feet above sea level. But not me;

I found a job and spent weekends hiking trails at elevations of up to 12,000 feet above sea level. It was glorious! I never had any altitude sickness, and in fact felt better than I ever had. Standing on a mountain trail with only my dog Phil back then was pure freedom. My lungs thrilled at the inhalation of mountain air, regardless of the elevation.

I've lived paycheck-to-paycheck most of my life. I have never regretted cashing in my profit sharing retirement fund to move to Colorado, even now that I've retired.

# 17

## Matchmakers at My Yard Sale

Before my move to Colorado, a couple in their 80s came to my yard sale and purchased some metal shelves. Too big to fit in their vehicle, the gentleman asked for a screw driver and pliers and began removing screws and bolts. This would take hours. My friend of ten years helped me at the yard sale. He kindly offered to deliver the shelves in his truck to their home if I went with him.

At the end of the yard sale, I went with my friend to deliver the shelves to the couple's house. The wife invited me in as the men carried the shelves into the garage. The wife asked a question about my friend, referring to him as my husband. I laughed and remarked that we were only friends. The wife quickly responded, "He looks at you with love." Again, I laughed off her comment, but paused to see if I could see what she saw.

In their garage was a pristine two-seater sports car, first generation MR2. We admired it and asked if it was for sale. The couple said they had considered selling it and offered for us to take it for a drive. After second visit to take the car for spin, my friend arranged to buy the car.

The husband and wife were determined matchmakers. When I drove him over to pick up the car after purchasing it, they invited us in to visit. Both seemed to have twinkles in their eyes as they smiled at each other. As the men discussed the car details in the garage, the wife brazenly challenged me to see that there was in fact more than friendship to our relationship. This time I did not laugh, rather I slowly contemplated the idea.

He drove his new sports car back to my house, and we sat on the back porch steps sharing the not-so-subtle comments the husband and wife had made to us separately. I expected him to laugh or make an objection, but he didn't do either. In fact, he gave me a long, thoughtful look.

How had I so blindly missed what the old couple promptly saw? I cherished our friendship and after many failed relationships, I did not want to jeopardize this friendship. The movie "When Harry Met Sally" provided food for our consideration that there may be more than friendship between us. Could my love for him be more than platonic? The greatest compliment I can offer is respect. My admiration and respect for his intelligence and integrity were genuine. I had observed his sacrifices over the years as a divorced father to ensure he had equal time with his son.

Our first awkward kiss was in the sports car.

After dating for a while, I decided I wanted us to be just friends, as we were still raising our sons. We had different ideas about parenting which caused some conflict. It takes a lot of commitment to go from a romantic relationship back to friends. Somehow we succeeded until...

...I moved to Colorado where I planned to stay for the rest of my life. Of all the people I knew, he was the only one who genuinely stayed in touch with me. I went back to Ohio for a visit, and on the last day we had dinner. The spark was undeniable. Within four months, after living in Colorado for one year, I moved back to Ohio in the summer. We were married the following spring on April Fool's Day.

The more I got to know myself, the more I knew I wanted a husband who is intelligent and has integrity. I wanted a man who would protect me and encourage me. We took the Myers-Briggs Personality Test as part of a healthcare seminar we attended. We learned his personality as an ISTJ, Introverted, Thinking, Judging, Sensing, compliments my ENFP personality, Extroverted, Intuition, Feeling, Perception. It makes for fun and sometimes deep conversations. After twenty plus years together despite numerous challenges we still respect and love each other.

My husband generously gives me gifts for all the holidays, more than making up for all the ones I missed as a child and young adult. One of my favorite gifts is a pair of earrings from National Geographic called Rainbow Seeds.

# 18

## Suicide

*I thought this chapter would be the shortest...*

Suicide has too often been in my thoughts when I felt worthless and unloved, especially when I was disfellowshipped. Kids of Jehovah's Witnesses grow up certain that if we ever mess up, our parents will abandon us - we will be dead to them. It's scary because we've seen it happen. Being disfellowshipped and shunned is supposed to make a person miss their family so much that they'll come back. I did miss my family and did what was necessary to be reinstated when I was nineteen. And then I didn't do what was necessary to continue to be a Witness when I was twenty-nine.

Some experts estimate the suicide rate of Jehovah's Witnesses to be five to ten times that of the general population. It is impossible to know exact numbers as hospitals and police departments don't record the religious affiliation of suicides.

For me the idea of suicide was to stop the pain and noise telling me I am of no value or worth. Having my family and all the Witness folks I thought loved or cared about me then reject me was devastating. Without spoken words I heard the noise of their condemnation. Being disfellowshipped also cancels any hope of love or everlasting life in Paradise.

When my first husband left, I wanted the pain to stop and yet at the same time knew I couldn't leave my sons. There was one incident after the divorce when I took off and drove to Colorado feeling overwhelmed, worthless, and unloved looking for a mountain where I could end it all. I couldn't. I was gone a few days and it took all my strength to return home. I walked into the door of my parents' home, who were watching my sons. I didn't receive a welcome and hugs. My father sternly said, "The next time you decide to take off, let us know." I was already ashamed of my behavior and weakness and left as soon as I could gather my sons' things. I never took off again.

When my sons were 16 and 18 years old I went into an acute depression. My family doctor wanted to prescribe antidepressants, but I refused thinking it showed weakness. He asked me to at least return to the psychologist I had seen years earlier. I made an appointment with her and she immediately recognized the depression. She guided me to the feelings deeply buried from my teens and my current feelings of being a failure as a mother when I saw my sons hurting.

When I saw her eight years earlier to get deprogrammed there were so many years of experiences, so much I never processed and so many feelings and tears I had never shed. The deep feelings of betrayal and worthlessness I had when I was the same ages of my sons now weighed me down. I could barely get out of bed in the morning and often went to work late, feeling the pressure that if I didn't work we wouldn't have money to live. Dr. Laura convinced me to get on antidepressants and continue therapy. It worked, as I dug myself out of another deep hole. It took over six weeks for the antidepressants to begin to kick in and with therapy my depression slowly lifted. I am thankful the doctors I worked for were patient and caring during my weeks of recovery.

Brief thoughts of suicide quickly pass now when words and actions of my dearest loved ones hurt me. It is easier to cry when someone me shows kindness and compassion. Tears that need to be cried hesitate or are held back when I am hurt and most need to shout out.

I knew a lovely, sweet young lady, one of Jehovah's Witnesses, who committed suicide. I truly believe she would be alive if she could have had counseling. I knew the Jehovah's Witness parents of a teenage boy, who committed suicide.

Suicide of course knows no religion. I also worked with a shy, bright Catholic lady whose brother committed suicide. She believed he had no chance to go to heaven because his last act was to take his life.

At the time I was enrolled in a Catholic University and researched the topic. I shared with her that in the 1990s, Pope John Paul II approved the Catechism of the Catholic Church, which acknowledged the role that mental illnesses may play in suicide. It was noted that grave psychological disturbances, anguish, or grave fear of hardship, suffering, or torture can diminish the responsibility of the one committing suicide. Catholics should not despair of the eternal salvation of persons who have taken their own lives. By ways known to God alone, God can provide the opportunity for repentance. The relief on her face as I shared this information, I remember to this day.

Years before I worked with her, I was working in the office of a doctor who was also the coroner of a very poor county. He was called to the home of a teenage boy who committed suicide with a shotgun. The death certificate read, Cause of Death: Suicide. The boy's Catholic parents called repeatedly asking for the death certificate to say it was an accident. The impact of beliefs profoundly scars lives.

My Mom...

One of Mom's dearest friends brought her to my home in Colorado. I didn't tell my sons their grandmother was coming. After traveling through a heavy snow storm in late October, they arrived late at night. There was a knock on our door, and I asked my sons to answer, feigning "It's probably a neighbor needing help." The absolute joy and surprise on her grandsons' faces lifted Mom above the clouds. We all hugged and laughed.

The next day my sons took Mom for a walk. Her friend confided to me that Mom had sat in her garage with the car running. Years of depression and being berated took its toll on a woman we loved. Mom would never get mental health counseling, so I spent time with her, gently using the questions and words I learned from my psychologists and my own experiences.

At the time I was taking an evening writing class at Fort Lewis College. The beautiful campus sits on a mesa overlooking historic Durango and the southern Rocky Mountains, and some days it is in the clouds. I took Mom with me. She had only completed two years of high school. Her mother died when she was only four years old. She grew up poor and went to work at an early age to help her family. Mom was concerned about going with me as she had never attended a college class. I assured her she would fit right in. Our assignment that night was cutting photos and words from magazines to tell a story. Mom was embraced by all as she related a funny story.

After class we sat in the parking lot and she opened up to share dreams she was never able to realize. I asked her why she never left her husband, and she said, "I had five kids, and in life you just trade one set of problems for another. I knew how to deal with the hand I had." We talked as close friends.

I stayed close to her with phone calls when she returned home. We spoke of her feelings and her favorite subjects: her children, grandchildren, and great-grandchildren. Mom was still one of Jehovah's Witnesses, who would have condemned her if they knew she had attempted suicide.

Below are my affectionate remembrances of my mother at her funeral almost fifteen years later:

> *My mother is an extraordinary woman. I first realized she was an extraordinary and extraordinarily happy woman—not just my mother—in August 1966 when I was twelve years old. Sometimes a memory is like a photograph or a short video clip. This memory is like a short video.*

> *It was late afternoon the last week in August. School would start after Labor Day, so I was thinking about how to enjoy every minute left of summer. We*

*lived on Fox Avenue, and I was outside on the back porch husking sweet corn. Dad would bring twelve dozen ears of corn home after work, and I would count them as I husked because Dad would ask me how many there were when he got home the next day. I happily finished the last batch and brought the corn with my little sister into the kitchen. My older sister was standing at the table cutting cooked corn off the cob and putting it into square plastic freezer containers. There were canners on the stove with boiling water. Tomatoes ripen at the same time as corn, so Mom was also canning bushels of tomatoes. My little sister was allowed to help with some tasks, as long as she was away from the dangers of the hot stove. My little brother had been outside with me and came inside to play in the living room with his Matchbox cars. My other brother, the baby, not yet two years old, was napping.*

*I could not see Mom's face when I walked in because her back was to me as she poured boiling water from a canner into the sink. Steam rose up all around her as did the food production in her kitchen. It was August, and we didn't have air conditioning, so Mom's hair curled even more than usual.*

*On my mind was how to get Mom to take us to Lake Isabella one more time before school started after Labor Day. But, of course I was waiting for the right moment to ask her, and since we were almost finished with a good day's work, I thought it was a good time. Something stopped me in that moment and I looked at her back and listened to her.*

*Mom was doing the thing she did so beautifully when she was happy, working hard, and everything was going well. She whistled a merry tune. Now Mom could really whistle a whole song, and if you knew the words, you could sing along, as she did not miss a note.*

*I saw her in that moment, not just as my mother, but as a woman, happy to have her five children by her side and her day's work nearly finished preserving foods for the winter ahead. At least, that's what I thought then.*

*As an adult looking back, I wonder if what she was happy about was also counting the days until school started when four of her five kids would be in school, and she would be home with the baby who still took naps.*

*Mom would say the thing in her life she was most proud of was her children. She taught us by word and by deed to start and finish a job and to do so with pride and precision. The other day, when Mom was feeling maudlin or sad, she told me that her pies were not really that good. I, of course, said, "Are you kidding me?" Her family, friends, and even casual acquaintances, would anxiously await a piece or even a crumb of her pie. Her children would fight over the last piece—make that a crumb—of her cinnamon piecrust roll. Her pies were special because she made them from scratch with love. She mixed up the crust with the recipe in her head and worked and rolled the crust just right. It takes me longer to find a Marie Callender crust in my freezer than for Mom to make one. She picked the berries, sliced the apples or peaches, and mixed just the right amount of sugar to sweeten, flour to thicken, and salt to flavor. My older sister would tease Mom that her crusts were better because she used Crisco or Pillsbury flour. We all knew no one could make a better pie than Mom. At potlucks and reunions, we who loved her pies, went to the dessert table first and her pie pans were the first ones emptied.*

*It was more than the ingredients and the mixing. It was the love and attention she gave to all her work. Whether she was baking a pie, making and serving a hot Black Midnight Cake with hot Seven Minute frosting, painting or wallpapering a room, Mom took pride and precision in all her relationships and work.*

*The Black Midnight Cake was a creation, and she was the artist and Cake Engineer. It consisted of three layers, and the icing was finished cooking just as she pulled the cakes from the oven. She precisely cut off the tops of two layers and began to build this masterpiece. Looking on at the cake building when my head was barely up to the kitchen counter, I watched her hands—and well, the cake. Anxiously awaiting the first hot bites, we probably looked like hungry animals circling their prey. As I grew older, I watched her face instead, as she took pride in her work, and she enjoyed the pleasure we all had devouring it.*

*How extraordinary for her to become such a wonderful mother when her mother died when she was only four years old. Her father died when she was only 28 years old, and over the years she lost all but one of her beloved brothers and sisters, and many of her nieces, relatives, and friends.*

*Mom lives on through her children, grandchildren, and great-grandchildren who enjoyed the fun activities she shared with them. She would put bicycles in her trunk and load up the car with grandkids to bike the trails at Blacklick and Dillon and others nearby parks. Croquet and badminton were in the backyard and a Ping-Pong and small used pool table in the basement. Swimming at Lake Isabella and vacations to the beach and mountains are treasured moments. One day while playing baseball, she was hit with a ball and got a black eye, yet continued to enjoy the day and even make homemade ice cream. She cheered at football, baseball, basketball, and soccer games, recitals, and graduations of her grandchildren. Feeding the birds in her yard and marking the names of the birds in her Audubon book with her grandchildren were special days. Card games, puzzles, and board games were favorites on rainy or cold days.*

*Throughout her life, Mom enjoyed helping others. She was an expert and tireless painter, wallpaper hanger, and decorator. Without any marketing efforts, she was sought after and busier than she ever expected, and often worked for free when someone needed help. She had an amazing ability with electrical and mechanical devices, once taking apart the back of the refrigerator to repair it herself.*

*Travel was one of her greatest pleasures. She enjoyed visiting and seeing how the local people lived more than the tourist attractions. Whether on a cruise, visiting Europe, or somewhere in Dresden, Ohio the trip was an adventure in which she desired to see new things and new people.*

*Her Apperson family reunion was a favorite annual event for her. She knew everyone and spoke with them about what was going on in their lives since she last saw them the year before. Her genuine interest, concern, and laughter flowed throughout Cy Young Park.*

*Laughter! Mom loved to hear and share a good joke with a twinkle in her eye and her ornery grin. Her motto was to "choose to be happy regardless of the pain, tears, or illness life brings." She was never a whiner. One of her neighbors, only a few hours before Mom passed away last Friday, thought Mom only had a broken arm.*

*Mom had suitcases full of photographs; postcards; greeting cards; news clippings; and graduation, wedding, and anniversary announcements which she loved to look at and share on the rare days weather kept her inside. It was no surprise I couldn't find a photograph of one of her pies because we were all too busy eating them.*

*She lived life with her arms and heart wide open…*

*A grateful daughter*

# 19

## Career then College

Attending a summer school class after my junior year of high school, gave me enough credits to graduate without requiring a senior year. I couldn't see any benefit in another of year of horticulture at the vocational school. My father's refusal to allow me return to high school for college prep classes eliminated that option. I didn't have a photo in the school yearbook and didn't attend graduation. Uneventfully, I picked up my diploma from the school office.

So before my 17th birthday I began working full-time. Initially, I worked for a flower shop for one dollar an hour at 40 hours a week. The small fortune allowed me to buy a used car- and after much pleading with my father to co-sign a loan, he relented. He seemed to enjoy me going to him with *please* and telling me *no*. Tears only made him angrier. He placed restrictions on my use of the car and demanded that it be available if he or my mother needed it.

I proudly drove the car home and parked it in front of the house. I was eager to drive it to work the next day. My shiny blue 1966 Chevelle Malibu was to become a little piece of freedom. My father informed me that my mother would need the car the next day. Once again, a small dream crushed.

After a few weeks at the flower shop, the owner's husband sent me to the basement to take inventory. Their only other employee was down there as well. He was in his thirties, married, with two children, and had worked for them for several years. Taking me to the far corner of the building, the employee started to attack me. I said I would scream, and he said they wouldn't hear me upstairs. So I said I would knock pottery pots and glass vases off the shelf. It worked. He angrily stopped, and I never spoke to anyone about the incident.

Looking to leave the flower shop and get a better job, it was recommended I go to one of the local hospitals for work. Better pay and the ability to apply for transfers to other departments seemed like a good move. The best opening at the time was a job in the kitchen assisting with cooking, baking, serving and delivering meals to patients in the hospital. A physical was required before I could start working, and I quickly scheduled the appointment.

A well-known obstetrician/gynecologist, with a nurse in the room, performed the pre-employment physical examination.

The nurse took my temperature, blood pressure, and pulse. The doctor came in and examined my eyes, ears, nose and mouth, then listened to my heart and lungs. After finishing, he told the nurse she could leave. As soon as the door closed, he had me lie back on the exam table, and he opened the front of the paper gown. I sensed something was not right. He told me I needed to learn how to do breast exams. He touched all around my breasts and nipples for some time. Years later, I learned his exam was not a typical breast exam. It seemed to be for his pleasure and maybe to elicit a sexual response from me. It did not. But once again, I told no one.

A pharmacy technician position opened up at the hospital, and I applied. Homemaking, required in school, was my least-liked subject, and I felt the same in my new position in the hospital kitchen. After nearly throwing up over a pan of sauerkraut, the personnel department helped me move to the job in the pharmacy. It was a newly created position for a narcotic control clerk and pharmacy technician to assist pharmacists with inventories and filling prescriptions, syringes, and deliveries to hospital floors. I loved the professional atmosphere and was eager to be trained. I was curious about medications and asked many questions. The pharmacists seemed to enjoy sharing their knowledge with me.

The nurses on the floors took their responsibilities seriously, as we inventoried their locked cabinets together. Dispensing narcotics required the name of each patient and dose given as well as the ordering physician name and the nurse issuing the dose. Each floor kept a supply of narcotics for emergencies and for use during the hours the pharmacy was closed. Nurses would put in requests for narcotic refills, and I was required to look at their records before I could deliver refills.

As a narcotic control clerk, I inventoried narcotics stored in the walk-in double-locked vault in the basement pharmacy. This was long before computers, so each drug had a paper inventory sheet. I counted all scheduled class drugs such as tablets, capsules, liquids, and even weighed pure cocaine crystals. I took my responsibilities seriously and was glad my work was reviewed by a pharmacist. Every dose taken from the vault required the signature of a pharmacist noted on the inventory log.

One day a staff pharmacist watched me inventory, including placing pure cocaine crystals on the scale to weigh them. He told me I needed to try cocaine and pressured me to place a tiny crystal on my tongue. He said it would not be missed. I pleaded with him that I could not risk losing my job. After his pressure and persistence, I gave in to the tiniest amount. The feeling was euphoric, and fortunately brief He asked me how I felt and I was terrified he would continue to pressure me to do it again, but he did not. Once again, I kept silent, as I knew it was more likely that between the two of us, I would lose my job and not him. A few years later he left the hospital, started a private pharmacy, and was rumored to be a drug addict.

I relished my time with pharmacists, physicians, and nursing professionals. They encouraged me to become a pharmacist based on my ability to learn quickly, ask perceptive questions, and my years of taking Latin with hopes of going to college.

The origin of Rx as an abbreviation for prescription is attributed to the Latin word *recipe*, which means *take*. Latin terms and acronyms were used to communicate when and how many doses were prescribed, *ac (ante cibum)* means before meals; *bid (bis in die)* means twice a day; *gt (gutta)* means drop; *hs (hora somni)* means at bedtime; *od (oculus dexter)* means right eye; *os (oculus sinister)* means left eye; *po (per os)* means by mouth; *pc (post cibum)* means after meals; *prn (pro re nata)* means as needed; *q3h (quaque 3 hora)* means every 3 hours; *qd (quaque die)* means every day; *qid (quater in die)* means 4 times a day.

While the Latin terms are still used by some doctors, these old terms are being replaced by orders in plain language.

Improved readability helps prevent medication errors and mix-
ups. It was recommended that prescribers write out instructions,
rather than use abbreviations. For example, prescribers would
write *daily* rather than *qd*, the abbreviated Latin term for every
day. In this case, *qd* could easily be misinterpreted as *qid* which
means 4 times a day or *od* which means right eye. Reading
doctors' handwriting on prescription pads was often a challenge.
Now with electronic health records, there is e-prescribing
(electronic prescribing), which adds another level of
improvement to the clarity of prescribing medications. How I
would have loved the ability to become a pharmacist.

After a while, a new pharmacy director started. He
treated me with respect and recommended me for more duties
within the pharmacy. I worked diligently and looked for
opportunities to learn and do more. Under a sterile air flow hood,
I filled syringes with unit doses of morphine and meperidine
from vials. A pharmacist would look at each syringe.

One time he found a small piece of rubber from the base
of the syringe. It had come from inside the large syringe I used to
withdraw the liquid narcotic, and then place the small dose into
the unit dose syringe through the rubber in the bottom. The
needle had nicked a piece of rubber. I was distraught and near
tears thinking I could have hurt a patient. He calmed me,
explaining the seriousness, but that it was his responsibility to

review and dispense to the patient. In the future I exercised even more caution and if a piece broke off, I put the syringe to the side for the pharmacist to review and sign off the dose on the inventory. Years later, prefilled unit dose syringes were made by pharmaceutical companies for hospitals to use.

The wife of the new pharmacist interviewed for a marketing position in the hospital and was accepted. It was whispered through the pharmacy department that she had experienced an unprofessional breast exam. It sounded like the same one I had. She immediately went to her husband and filed a complaint. The suspected doctor kept his privileges to admit and care for his patients in the hospital, but was relieved of his duties to do pre-employment physical examinations. Six years after my pre-employment physical, the same doctor almost cost me the life of my first baby and myself.

I enjoyed my work in the pharmacy and knew the limitations of my position. One day, a doctor near retirement asked me to run his office. He was an Internal Medicine physician specializing in Black Lung Disease. He had previously retired from the military and had worked as an expert in forensic pathology which focuses on determining the cause of death by examining a corpse. He played the role of an advisor in the sensational death of a woman drowning in a car in Massachusetts. I was fascinated by his stories.

The practical and first-hand education he and his wife, a nurse, provided about medical office management gave me a solid base for a new career. I read everything I could get my hands on in order to be the best. Doctors I worked with shared their copies of Medical Economics and encouraged me to attend educational meetings and join local and national associations of healthcare business professionals.

After moving to the big city, I looked for and found a newly forming local Medical Office Manager group. I was asked to join their board and gladly accepted, serving for many years. I was happy to be part of a group of people I respected.

Healthcare management was a great fit and opportunity for me. I liked studying and researching in order to be current on all matters. It was a time of tremendous changes in healthcare particularly with managed care plans and government regulations emerging. I became an expert on Operations Management, Financial Management, Human Resource Management, Organizational Governance, Risk and Compliance Management, and later Patient-Centered Care and electronic health records.

A short time after joining the local group, I became aware of a state group and their national organization of medical practice executives. I served on the State Board at all levels, even rising to President. I am most proud of achieving

Certification as a Medical Practice Executive. I had only taken a handful of college classes over the years at community and state colleges. The Certification test was given to people, most with Master's Degrees, accountants, and a few doctors. One of the doctors I worked with wrote a letter to recommend me for the exams. I was treated as an equal, even though I did not have a college degree. A respected healthcare executive told me I have a practical master's degree. I really appreciated his comment. After passing the exams I became their state representative for the American College of Medical Practice Executives. As a Jehovah's Witness woman I would not have been allowed in any leadership role. Achieving career success as a female executive in a male dominated field was especially gratifying.

There were three exams for certification: oral, essay, and objective questions. The first time I took the exams I rolled right along, confident in the objective and essay sections. The oral exam became a trauma. I sat in front of three certified members who were instructed to be stoic and not show the examinee any sign of whether their answers are right or wrong. Besides looking for the correct answers, a level of professionalism is also expected by the panel members. I walked into the room confidently and was asked a series of questions for scenarios to which I knew the answers. I was doing great! Then about two-thirds of the way to finishing, I suddenly froze. I asked a member to repeat their question, and my mind went blank. I instantly became the terrified 18-year-old girl sitting in front of three elders judging me. I couldn't finish. The look on my face must have frightened the examiners, as it did a close associate who saw me walking back to the main exam room. I couldn't speak.

I passed the objective questions but needed to retake the essay portion as my answers were correct but too short. I also needed to retake the oral examination portion in order to become certified. One of my buddies who took the exams practiced with me sitting in front of her. She was my friend, so it was easy to answer. The next time I sat again in front of three examiners, I thought of her. I passed. I am more proud of that certification, which I achieved through my hard work and practical efforts, than my college degree which occurred ten years later.

I maintained my certification for many years including 50 hours of continuing education every three years. I was studying many more hours than required, as I wanted to be current and keep up with more academically educated associates.

The national organization had regional and national conferences where I learned so much. Some attendees skipped session, while I planned in advance how to attend as many as possible. There was time allocated to visit vendors, and I took a great interest in electronic technologies. The electronic health record and interconnectivity of medical office and hospitals was developing. One of my favorite jobs before retiring was being a regional director bringing new technologies for healthcare into Appalachian counties. I worked with hospitals, community health centers, and medical offices of primary care and specialties. My favorites were the solo practice primary care physicians and their staff in rural and often poor communities. These folks were especially amazing and gracious.

Due to the large size of the conferences, they were held in major cities. I was able to visit places like San Francisco, San Diego, Denver, New Orleans, Boston, San Antonio, Orlando, and others. The physicians in the medical offices where I worked paid for me to attend. I could never afford to go on my own. Whenever possible I carved out a few hours or an extra day to see the sites.

In San Francisco I was able to rent a car and drive the crookedest street and across the Golden Gate Bridge into the Napa Sonoma wine country. Muir Woods along the California coast was one of the most extraordinary places I ever saw, a pristine forest of coastal redwoods peaceful and beautiful. I hiked up a trail and, forgetting to take water with me I drank from a spring at the top of the hill.

In San Diego I saw beautiful sandy beaches and enjoyed sunny weather and delicious seafood. It was an exceptional place, apart from the earthquake with a magnitude of 7.1 which rolled me out of bed on the 23rd floor of the hotel in the middle of the night. We were advised to take the stairs to the lobby and then went outside in case of aftershocks. After a short time we took the stairs back to the room where the walls only had small cracks near the ceiling. An unplanned adventure.

Over the years I have been a speaker at local, regional, and national conferences. I am amazed I was able to teach and train medical students in a university setting about electronic health records and other technologies.

I served on Committees with the AMA Accelerating Change in Medical Education, Informatics and Technology Committee; Board Member of the Appalachian Health Information Exchange; Federal EHR Incentive Payment for Ambulatory Practitioners; and HIMSS Meaningful Use Center of Excellence Work Group.

I learned to be assertive in my career, the first office I managed after moving to Columbus affectionately called me boss and later chief. My first email name, suggested to me by a computer consultant, was MsChief. I was no longer a Miss or Mrs. and the term Ms., pronounced Mizz, was popular in the 1980s. My titles were a far cry from the submissive and passive women of Jehovah's Witnesses.

Finally at the age of 52, I finished my undergraduate degree with a Bachelor of Science in Business Management and was Magna Cum Laude. I attended commencement and was so incredibly proud of finishing, which would never be possible under the watchful eyes of elders and Jehovah's Witnesses. My parents did not attend or celebrate my commencement. Two years after retiring, I finally paid off all my student loans.

Today the bumper sticker on my three-wheeled trike reads, "It's never too late to be a cowgirl."

# 20

## Granny and Granny 2.0

### Berry Patches

Her armor extra layers of heavy leggings, sweaters, and boots.

The goal she fought for, berries: sweet, ripe, ready to be picked.

Prepared for enemies: briars, thorns, and insects she went up the hill.

The cool, early, barely lit quiet morning hours, with dew covering the vines,

ready for battle.


Each basket filled with berries, a prize; our sense of accomplishment.

There will be fresh jellies, pies, and cobblers today.

Feeling light, carefree. Successfully we march on.

A sudden movement to her left catches my eye. Hers, too, as she moves swiftly.

My memory sees the scene in slow motion.

With the rake, a snake is killed, tossed aside. She resumes picking.

My mouth opened I am motionless, in awe of her courage.

A hero, a knight in armor, fearless.

As the shock wears off, I babble to her;

a nervous child, fearful another dragon will appear.

Calm, she encourages me to continue unafraid.

My head held higher, my shoulders back, my sense of self, strong and confident.

She explained different types of snakes, friendly and unfriendly.

Enemies and heroes come in different packages.

Tiny, under five feet, a hero stood before me.


The hands which picked and killed, comforted.
Brushing my hair, gently placing drops of warm, sweet oil
in my aching ears.

Rosewater and glycerin, her smell.

Peanut butter cupcakes with peanut butter icing baked in an old oven, burned the bottoms.

"They taste best that way…"

Gardens with vegetables and flowers fill her yard.

Deluxe outhouse, a two-seater, with urinal, locking Keren in.

Spring water well and goldfish.

Small red boxes of pretzels and penny candy hidden in her pantry.

Gifts for grandchildren, great-grandchildren.


Walks through the cemetery, stories of family, friends, and past loves.

Pieces of wood with plastic flowers and animals for graves.

A son, a husband lie and wait.

Heroes are human.

Now an adult, different enemies appear; some ignored, some eliminated.

The lesson remains.

On a Greenwood hill, she protects and encourages me.

Spunky, gentle, unassuming, proud.

Sylvia: mother, grandmother, great grandmother, friend, brave lady.

Always with me.

January 1994


My tiny grandmother looked ten feet tall to me as a child and as an adult. She was tenacious in a quiet, unassuming way. I wrote the poem above when she died to express my love and admiration for her.

When my first grandbaby was born, my second son and his wife asked what I would prefer to be called. My little sister had years earlier embraced the sweet name Mimi. Without hesitation I said, "Granny." I hope all my grandchildren love and respect me as much as I loved and respected my only Granny.

## 21

# Impact of Beliefs and I Found You Jimmy

Asking questions about beliefs, studying religions, and visiting places of worship is a lifelong quest for me. After leaving the cult of Jehovah's Witnesses, I never joined another organized religion. My oldest son says my beliefs have been a moving target.

I asked him, "What do you believe?"

He stated, "My moral compass is good. My personal integrity is good."

As a Witness everything was good or bad. Forbidden sins, evil and anyone who is not a Jehovah's Witnesses is bad and referred to as the world or worldly people. Jehovah, his faithful Witnesses and their truths are good. I challenge the black and white of religious beliefs, when I have seen all the colors of gray within.

As I researched how cults start, there seems to me a kind of formula. A man, generally, develops a reason to question beliefs or disagree with another man or church and subsequently comes up with his own ideas. Then he seeks out followers spinning his beliefs for his own benefit. Cult leaders must be charismatic and magnetic to draw followers.

According to the Encyclopaedia Britannica, the name: *Jehovah* is the artificial Latinized rendering of the name of the God of Israel. The name arose among Christians in the Middle Ages through the combination of the consonants YHWH (JHVH) with the vowels of *Adonai* (My Lord). Jews reading the Scriptures aloud substituted *Adonai* for the sacred name, commonly called the tetragrammaton.

For me the name Jehovah came to mean a cruel god exacting punishment for human mistakes and tearing apart families.

I have visited numerous Christian churches, a Buddhist temple, and a Jewish synagogue and while living in Colorado, Native American services, as well as a service at a rodeo. I hesitated before walking alone into an outside Cowboy Church. The first words to reach my ears were how Jesus didn't always get along with his parents. The minister related the story when Jesus was twelve and stayed at the temple for days and his parents had to look for him. He said no matter whether we are teens or adults, in all situations Jesus understands us and to approach, not timidly, but boldly to receive the grace of God. In the final benediction he read a poem with a line, cowboys loop your rope for Jesus. It still makes me smile.

To finally finish my undergraduate degree as an adult taking night classes, I attended a private Catholic liberal arts university. I most appreciated learning about the different Bibles, books, and Catholic beliefs.

My chosen daughter attended an Episcopal Seminary and shared enlightening information with me as well. I loved our conversations as we explored beliefs and philosophies. Visiting her and being in the beautiful peaceful church at the seminary in rural Tennessee warmed my heart. Today she is a priest in an old church in New England which is lovely with its wood and glass architecture and welcoming atmosphere.

Mentioning architecture, I immediately remember the Sistine Chapel and St. Peter's Church in Rome when my husband and I toured Italy for our tenth anniversary. We visited museums and churches and were awed by their grandeur. However, we saw nothing as opulent as Vatican City. Seeing only a fraction of the riches during our tour, I had to wonder how many lives it cost to obtain the wealth, and how many lives today could be improved by extending their riches to feed, house, and educate the poor and heal the sick.

Searching the internet I submitted the question, "How many religions are there in the world in 2020?" One site stated, "A religion is defined as a system of faith or worship. A religious person believes in a higher power, such as a God or Gods. Beliefs vary based on religion."

Adding, "There are many different religions, but the most popular is Christianity, followed by an estimated 33% of people; and Islam, which is practiced by over 24% of people. Other religions include Hinduism, Buddhism, and Judaism. Of course, there is also a large population – about 1.2 billion people worldwide – that are nonreligious or have Atheist beliefs."

Thereafter, it lists the following for each religion's total world population:

Christianity - 2.38 billion

Islam - 1.91 billion

Hinduism - 1.16 billion

Buddhism - 507 million

Folk Religions - 430 million

Other - 61 million

Unaffiliated - 1.19 billion

My next question is, *What do these religions say about what happened to Jimmy?* Researching books and the internet, I have attempted to answer the question. I apologize for any errors in my interpretations.

Christianity:

o  Most believe that God claims ownership of all children in the world though all time regardless of being the children of believers or non-believers.

o  God always shows compassion to His innocent ones. All children who die are welcomed in the presence of the Lord and live with Him eternally in heaven.

o  Adults who repent of their sins and trust in Jesus Christ will be eternally reunited with their precious little ones.

Islam:

o  According to the Quran and the sayings of the Prophet, children of believers who die before reaching the age of puberty will live in Paradise, and the children of non-Muslims who die will also live in Paradise.

o  It is by Allah's justice that He saves the children of unbelievers from the Hellfire because they are originally born pure and innocent.

Hinduism:

o  All Hindus believe that life, death, and rebirth are a continuous process that all are part of.

Buddhism:

o   Buddhists believe life is in a cycle of death and
     rebirth, and when someone dies their energy passes
     into another form as a human, animal, or even
     ghosts, demi-gods, or gods.

o   Good actions will result in a better rebirth, while bad
     actions will have the opposite effect.

o   Enlightened individuals who die reach Nirvana, no
     longer needing to be reborn.

Atheists:

o   Atheists believe when you die, it's over and you live
     on in the memory of the people you love and who
     loved you.

o   In spite of all the evils and problems in the world,
     they believe they are already living in heaven, and
     it's the heaven they work to make during their life
     on earth.

Universalists:

o   Many Universalists ascribe to the assumption that
     life does not continue after death, while others hold
     it as an open question, wondering if our minds will
     have any awareness when we are no longer living.

o  Few believe in divine judgment after death by
   rejecting the idea of eternal damnation.


Folk religions, others and unaffiliated propose numerous
beliefs of life and death.

Ultimately, places of worship are about people. As
humans we are imperfect and may look for forgiveness of our
mistakes. We may sincerely want to be a better person. Or, we
may want to look like we are trying to be a better person to
impress others by sitting in a service or attending church. One
thing I know is that all people make mistakes deliberately or
accidentally. Too often I have made decisions in haste with a
knee-jerk reaction to a situation and later regretted my choice. If
I knew then what I know now I would have made some better
choices. I suppose most people can agree.

Do I believe in God? Rather than say "God" or name a
god, I believe there must be a higher power. The God of
Jehovah's Witnesses, I do not believe in, as he is for me
unloving and judgmental, causing families to break apart.

**I found you, Jimmy.**

The headstone with the words "Our Son," his name, the few years he lived, and a small lamb mark Jimmy's grave. To the left, a larger headstone with the names of his maternal grandparents stands. The little cemetery rests on a rolling hill in a community of less than one hundred. A sign notes the first traffic fatality in the state in 1835 when a stagecoach rolled over when its horses were startled by a drove of pigs.

Finding his grave, even with the internet, proved a challenge. Locating the obituary from a local newspaper led me to the name of the funeral home and provided a starting point. Unfortunately, the funeral home could not provide the name of the cemetery. In the summer college students document graves on the website gravefinder.com, but I did not find any information for Jimmy's grave there. Traipsing through cemeteries in the general vicinity of his home, I filled hours searching and reflecting over the years.

Remembering the name of a nearby monument company, I called, and they had computerized records dating back all the years of their business. A kind lady provided me the name of the cemetery, the size and shape of the headstone and the inscriptions, making the search easier and ultimately successful.

Respectfully, walking between graves as my grandmother taught me and through multiple rows, I read tombstones. Often pausing when a name or date or unusual inscription caught my eye took more time. Nearing the end of the time I had allotted to search one day, it was almost unexpectedly before me.

After years of searching, there was Jimmy's grave. Initially, I felt elated to have found him. And then it surprised me to sob from almost sixty years of searching for him—and for me. The intensity of sorrow I felt as I looked at the aged headstone amid the green grass and remembered his sweet face brought me to the ground. Through tears I cried, "Jimmy, you are still alive in my heart. Wherever love goes after death, you are there. Thank you for helping me question and search for life's truths."

Fully aware his body in the grave had turned to dust, it was the realization of the impact his short life had on me that shook me so. I had not just been searching throughout my many years to literally find Jimmy, but I had been looking for conviction in my own beliefs, and not those taught to me by a cult as a child and young adult.

Memories of being unable to play with him for a while, and then the day of his funeral, replayed. There are so many what ifs. *What if he had contracted leukemia a few years later when a treatment and cure was beginning? What if his parents, who treated me with such tenderness, had remained in my life? What if the busy bodies didn't revel in judging and dismissing his life as if it were of no consequence?* All of the what ifs versus the what was and what is…

As his breath of life left his body, I believe his spirit soared. The moments of his gentleness remain in me. When someone is kind to me, I feel most deeply brought to tears. When someone is cruel, I am angry and stronger.

I continued to tell him, "Jimmy, your life and death mattered to me. The questions I asked, and the lessons I learned, and the life I lead… thank you." And I added, "I love you."

In his memory I plant blue bachelor buttons. The small bright flowers are a lovely reminder of his life.

Life is precious. Kindness is equally precious. Strength is required to survive life.

I'm calling this my final chapter only in reference to my book. I hope I have many healthy years ahead to continue to explore and search and be with my loved ones. There is so much more to read and learn and places to see. I respect the beliefs of my family and friends even when they differ from my own.

The picture on the seed packet of small, delicate, beautiful blue bachelor button flowers reminds me most of

Jimmy as I plant them each spring. I believe our breath of life, the spirit, the life-force within each person and each seed I plant is an energy existing before and after we live and for all time. The sweetness and innocence of Jimmy lives within every flower, butterfly, sunshine, rain drop and wherever there is a joyful thought.

Today my backyard serenity gardens are full of beautiful perennial and annual flowers. Myriads of daffodils and a few crocuses pop up through the snow in March or April as winter nears its end. In May and June, the sweet, almost grape-like smell of irises announces their tender lavender colors. These are followed by fragrant, bright pink, mauve, and white peonies.

With the warmth of June and July blooms of prickly pear cactus will open like bursts of sunshine. Each individual flower, adored by bees, only blooms yellow for one day. My cluster of cactus multiplies, as some flowers bloom at the same time and others in succession.

Finicky hydrangeas, based on soil content and weather extremes, exhibit different colors of blooms if and when they choose. Yellow, peach, and pink irises begin flowering in May and June with some showing their colors even in August and September.

Purple-pink coneflowers bloom June through August as butterflies and hummingbirds feed on the nectar. Birds eat the seeds after the flowers are spent. As their cones start to dry in the fall, I cut them off and save them for bird food throughout the winter.

Tiny wild black raspberries ripen on vines scattered erratically about our three acres in late June and early July. I sense my Granny beside me as I serenely pick them and gently place them into my basket.

Remembering Jimmy gives me a feeling of gratitude in my quest of my truths. An old and faded photograph of his sweet smile imparts a feeling of appreciation in the most precious moments. His short life, in terms of years, lives longer within my years, and hopefully moves beyond in the years of my loved ones.

As I near 70, I think about my passing and I want my ashes scattered about the earth to feed trees, plants, and mountain wildflowers. As my breath of life goes out into the universe, my place of worship, I want it to send it with love and kindness.

# About the Author

**Kathy Jefford** was born in the Southeastern Ohio Appalachian town of Zanesville in 1953. Her parents, devout Jehovah's Witnesses, raised her in their dedicated community of believers. Early in life, Kathy was stunned to lose a close childhood companion. Piercing questions shrouded the fate of his soul and sent her on a life-long search for answers. Six decades spent asking *Where's Jimmy*? led Kathy to discover and develop spiritual beliefs of her own.

Choosing authenticity in every aspect of her life cost Kathy every comfort and familiarity she had grown up knowing. Shedding staunch religious restrictions, male-dominated rules for women and society, and the simple luxury of questioning one's core values and belief system, Kathy broke free to make a life of her own. A pioneer in her family, her education, and her contributions in her health care career, Kathy simultaneously learned to write, knowing that one day she would fulfill her desire to share her story in hopes of encouraging others to find truth and freedom.

Now retired from the health care system, debut author, Kathy Jefford, lives on the edge of Ohio's Appalachian region with her husband, two German Shepherds, and ten chickens.

Made in the USA
Monee, IL
24 March 2022

0bb61126-bf9c-4351-84e6-71836104d4a1R01